Bid Me to Live

(A Madrigal)

H.D.

Bid Me
to Live

(A Madrigal)

The Dial Press
New York

Published by
The Dial Press
1 Dag Hammarskjold Plaza
New York, New York 10017

Cover photograph of H.D. c. 1923 by The
Estate of Man Ray; used with kind
permission of The Collection of American
Literature, Beinecke Rare Book and
Manuscript Library, Yale University, and by
The Estate of Man Ray.

Library of Congress Cataloging in Publication Data

H.D. (Hilda Doolittle), 1886–1961.
Bid me to live (a madrigal).

I. Title.
PS3507.0726B5 1983b   811'.52   83-1965
ISBN 0-385-27880-2

TO ANTHEA

Bid me to live, and I will live
   Thy Protestant to be:
Or bid me love, and I will give
   A loving heart to thee. . . .

Bid me to weep, and I will weep,
   While I have eyes to see:
And having none, yet I will keep
   A heart to weep for thee.

Bid me despair, and I'll despair,
   Under that cypress tree:
Or bid me die, and I will dare
   E'en Death, to die for thee.

Thou art my life, my love, my heart,
   The very eyes of me:
And hast command of every part,
   To live and die for thee.
                         Robert Herrick

I

Oh, the times, oh the customs! Oh, indeed, the times! The customs! Their own, specifically, but part and parcel of the cosmic, comic, crucifying times of history. Times liberated, set whirling out-moded romanticism; Punch and Judy danced with Jocasta and Philoctetes, while wrestlers, sprawling in an Uffizi or a Pitti, flung garish horizon-blue across gallant and idiotic Sir Philip Sidney-isms. It was a time of isms. And the Ballet.

They did not march in classic precision, they were a mixed bag. Victims, victimised and victimising. Perhaps the victims came out, by a long shot, ahead of the steady self-determined victimisers. They escaped; the rowdy actual lost generation was not actually their generation. They had roots (being in their mid-twenties and their very early thirties) still with that past. They reacted against a sound-board, their words echoed, were not lost in the drawl of later sirens. If Bella predicted that later film or stage-type, maybe Bella was ahead of them, more fashionable, then, the more de-

termined to self-destruction; it was not because Bella was so
actually of the lost, of that lost generation, it was simply
that Bella was anyway doomed to self-extinction. In any
time, lost, the harlot of the middle-age miracle-play, while
Julia was almost ridiculously some nun-figure, gaunt, over-
intellectualized, of the same play. But Bella was not a har-
lot, Julia was not a saint. When Rafe Ashton said to Julia,
"I would give her a mind, I would give you a body," he was
biting off, extravagantly, much more than even he could
chew.

Were they extrovert? Introvert? They had no names
for these things. True, the late war-intellectuals gabbled of
Oedipus across tea-cups or Soho café tables; it was not Vimy
or Loos they talked of. What was left of them was the war-
generation, not the lost generation, but lost actually in fact,
doomed by the stars in their courses, an actuality, holocaust
to Mars, not blighted, not anaemic, but wounded, but dy-
ing, but dead.

True, they were shoved about, flagrant pawns in a fla-
grant game; externally they found themselves in out-of-the-
way cottages, in a room in Kensington, in two rooms in
Hampstead, in a huge drawing-room in Bloomsbury. So-
and-so knows someone who has a cottage; won't you take it,
Frederick? As if she, Julia or he, Rafe or someone who had
met Bella's mother before they gave up their studio in Paris
had this right, this power—they were rich, in their way. Take
so-and-so's cottage, they have a cottage, a sort of lodge I be-
lieve, and it's empty and they asked me and Rafe to go there
before he went to France, seemed suitable introduction,

their sort of visiting-card on a silver tray. Frederick was a person. Already, too much a person. But the Americans who had the house, who had the lodge, wrote back politely and firmly that after all, wasn't Mrs Frederick a German? They forgot of course that Elsa was a German. And a slap in the face from people who wanted to meet people with whom she and Rafe and Morgan were on good terms, was a slap in the face; so, slapped in the face, we must remember that Elsa is a German.

Will you, won't you, will you, won't you, will you? Bella had flung in her lot with a war-battered minority (or majority). "I had lovers," she said; she sat on the chintz-covered couch that was one of the "pieces" that Miss Ames asked Julia if she minded. "I mean, do you mind," Miss Ames said, "if I leave them; it only means I have to store them, I haven't enough furniture for this room, anyhow no one wants this room, it's too cold. Mr Levsky said you might like this room." This was Miss Ames, early Fabian of the period, herself already period-piece in 1914, in 1917 already pre-war, valiant militant suffragette with brown velvet jacket. She was very tiny. Sometimes she wore her little George Sand jacket with trousers. Her hair was naturally curly, untidy but not dowdy. Mop of gold-brown hair went grey at the temples. Fine wrinkles etched blue eyes. She spoke precisely, with the indefinable *je ne sais quoi* of the aristocrat. "I don't like ugly women," she said, flicking ash from the end of amber.

Then there was the room. Chief in importance the room itself, the frame to the picture, the curtains that might at any moment part on carnage in Queen's Square. Three double rows of curtains hung in parallel pleats from curtain poles. Julia had hemmed them herself. Behind the curtains were thick double shutters with heavy iron bolts that they drew across in air-raids. "Not that it matters," said Miss Ames, "I've insured the place, it's the light. Please bolt the shutters." Then as an after-thought, as she turned the pseudo-Sand shoulder, "Oh, by the way, Mrs Ashton, wouldn't it be better if you did not take the room, after all? I have a friend, influential—I could get you out of town—"

Out of town?

They would get her out of town, they would save her, for what?

But she wasn't to be saved that way. She was in the middle of something. Three long French windows, three double sets of curtains that she had hemmed herself, were three symbolical sets of curtains about to part on carnage in Queen's Square. She could not know that she was in the middle of a trilogy, she could not phrase it that way. She was in the middle of something. They all were. That war.

Having stuck it one year, two years, the beginning of a third year, why should she give in now, go, as they urged her, back to America, go, as they suggested, into the country? *J'y suis.*

I myself, I myself, I myself. This is my room. What had happened the year before, the year before that, was hardly more than a reflection of a rim of a glass set down on a varnished table. A ring, a year, last year. Last year was already dimmed into vague reflections of memories, the cottage in Devonshire and Ivan Levsky cooking potatoes on an oil-stove. She had not liked Devon; already Frederick was writing, "Why don't you and Rafe come to Cornwall?" Rafe did not want to go to Cornwall, did not want to "get mixed up with the Fredericks." Maybe he did want to get mixed up with the Fredericks. Holding out against something that was later to be more completely shattered, as against something to be too early shattered. They were moved rather than moving, hedged in by comment, by precise and precisely aimed poisonous arrows, by words that meant nothing but that stung across all the surface of life; ambushed, they dodged.

Mrs Rafe Ashton. That is my name. It was a blithe arrangement. They might have made a signal success of their experiment. They made a signal success of it, but in the tradition not so much of Robert Browning and Elizabeth Barrett as of Punch and Judy. They both wanted to be free, they both wanted to escape, they both wanted a place where they could browse over their books; they had friends in common. They crawled under *Mercure de France*, barricaded themselves with yellow-backed French novels, Pindar in the original which they could not read (she picked out a word here, there, with a dictionary, he manipulated a telling phrase now and again), the Greek Anthology.

Superficially entrenched, they were routed out by the sound of air-craft; she stumbled down the iron stairs (that was the Hampstead flat) and bruised her knee. Just in time to see the tip-tilted object in a dim near sky that even then was sliding sideways and even then was about to drop. Such a long way to come. It drifted from their sight and the small collection of gaping individuals dispersed. Leviathan, a whale swam in city dusk, above suburban forests. My knee. It was a black gash, she might have broken her leg. Suddenly, as he filled a basin from the bathroom, her mind, which did not really think in canalized precise images, realized or might have realized that if she had had the child in her arms at that moment, stumbling as she had stumbled, she might have. . . No. She did not think this. She had lost the child only a short time before. But she never thought of that. A door had shuttered it in, shuttering her in, something had died that was going to die. Or because something had died, something would die. But she did not think that. And he lifted the slightly tainted bowl of water and said, "Poor Julia, poor Judy." And everything was where everything was and it doesn't matter that the *Lark* can't pay us for our translations any more and stopped Rafe's French Parnassian series, and the *Weekly* has been incorporated into something vaguely propagandish, and Rafe said he might as well enlist as give up his time to statistics, all humbug, he said. And she did not shout (how could she?) Oh, God, enlist then, go, go, go, go, go.

It was shut in her as other things were shut in her because "the war will be over." (The war will never be over.) I strove too high physically: "Now Mrs Ashton, you have such a nice body, you will always regret it if you do not have this child." Later, she took a room near Rafe (after he had enlisted) at Corfe Castle. But then he had not yet gone, and coming back with the towel still dangling from his arm, she said, "You look like a waiter with that towel dangling from your arm." Corfe Castle was after the child and they were just where they had been except for a gap in her consciousness, a sort of black hollow, a cave, a pit of blackness;

black nebula was not yet concentrated out into clear thought.

The surface was as the surface had been. Only colder. Only—but I waited for you to come back and then you will be careful but what good was that; shivering, she received the dregs of what had been, not openly resentful.

If the wound had been nearer the surface, she could have grappled with it. It was annihilation itself that gaped at her.

"I'm sorry," (as if that could possibly mean anything), "did I hurt you, Judy?"

But such a fear, even with complete detached psychological equipment, is not easily dealt with. Perhaps better no knowledge. This was no occasion for a little knowledge is a dangerous thing. The greater the gap in consciousness, the more black-hole-of-Calcutta the gap; the more unformed the black nebula, by reasoning, the more glorious would be the opening up into clear defined space, or the more brilliant a star-cluster would emerge, if somehow, at some time, the surface could be adequately dealt with. Sufficient unto the day. This was not that day. But the more she feared, repudiated Rafe in her black-Calcutta self, the more she strove to reach him.

This is our flat, this is our room, this is our bed. I mustn't get nervous, it will spoil everything, was (if any) the thought that sustained her as she crawled to the side of the bed. "Don't you think we might put on the kettle?"

He would do that, charming in deference.

II

He would come back, just as he always had done, while the kettle was coming to a boil on the gas-ring. And she would think (not thinking in these words) now for this moment, it's perfect. It will be perfect. She would find herself listening, as one listening far, far off, to echo of an echo; echo in a shell? What was she listening for? The preliminary cricket-trill of the kettle, just before it actually comes to a boil, she would tell herself. She was listening to his voice in his voice, a voice in a shell; his actual voice was coarsened, his throat hardened, but in his voice was his voice, echo. She was listening to that; she would hear that, that was the reason for her marriage, had been the reason of her near-death; the reason for her escape, emancipation, inspiration.

It was his voice. What he said might or might not be re-lated to his way of saying it, but she would listen to what he might be about to say, thinking all the time, it's very quiet, it must be about three or four. She might say, London is the quietest place in the world, once it is quiet. Might have added, after an air-raid, everything, once it is quiet, is a grave-yard; we walk among stones, paving-stones, but any stone might have been our tomb-stone, a slice of a wall falling, this ceiling over our heads. But she did not think that, could not of course say it, would not have said it, even if she had thought it clearly, for he was back from France.

He would be going back to France. To-morrow, to-day. They would brew tea (all this had happened before), they would find eggs in the shelf under the book-case where they kept their shoes. They would smoke, and while a winter-dawn stole over a sleeping city he would say those things that might (God knows) have better been left unsaid. If he had been the ordinary Englishman, he wouldn't have said them; but of course, if he had been the ordinary Eng-lishman, she wouldn't have married him. She had married him when he was another person. That was the catch, really.

She was listening to the sound in the shell, in the voice of the man beside her. She was listening, alert (propped on a somewhat spindly elbow) she thought, for the little cricket-chirp that the kettle gave out when the water was about to boil.

"You're trembling."
"No."
This was the witch's hour, this was the terrible moment when something was about to happen. Here, in this room with the gas-ring for some symbolic round-stone, and the kettle for some instrument of divine or diabolic interven-tion, something was about to happen. She recognized the symptoms, herself worn to a frazzle and her lank hair pushed

back from her "too high Flemish forehead" as (quoting
Pater) he liked to call it; something was bound to happen.
Not the physical over-sensual contact. Something else,
something not that, yet arising from that, another substance
but the same, as ice, as steam, as water are all the same yet
three states. So here. So now. Out of themselves, there
would be the ghost emanation, that would be—that would
be—"cigarette?" "Why, yes, yes—" And while he peered for
matches or with the familiar gesture slapped pockets (the
pocket of his camel-hair dressing-gown, then getting up, the
pocket of his khaki tunic) she knew the something was on
them. The thing they had between them, that they con-
jured up— "You are trembling."

"It's the way I crooked my elbow, you know, this way—
it's nothing—" She shook herself erect, sat upright on a bed,
that was marriage-bed, that was death-bed, that was resur-
rection.

Every cigarette, if you came to think of it, was conti-
nuity. Chain-smoking. Smoking now, to-night, this evening
(this morning) was ritual in sequence; the narcotic incense,
the dried crumbled leaf, was actually a leaf, grown with a
white flower. Actually, the symbol of this incense was white,
narcotic, a white flower. Oh, no, no, she did not see it, did
not make any such comparison in her mind, but that's what
it was. It was a white flower, pointed petals, white lotus if
you will, white anyhow. Some Buddhistic hangover from a
last-life, put it, if you deal in the occult, but she did not want
to merge off into any slip-shod way of thinking. It wasn't
that.

It was actual, yes, it actually was a glyph, traced in the air. That is, if you could take all that it symbolized, the khaki tunic flung over the back of the arm-chair, the webby bit of the camel-hair dressing-gown at his elbow, that had almost worn through, the rough camel-hair rope that he had tied around; Saint Anthony. Yes, he was Saint Anthony; what kind of a saint was she, or who? Claire? Mated, un-mated, two saints living in separate walled-in seclusion, would find the same answer in the up-rising incense, in a cold lady-chapel at dawn, as they found in a cold studio liv-ing-room in Bloomsbury, in Queen's Square, to be exact, the night before he was going back to France.

"It's boiling."

"Yes."

She was caught in the bed-clothes. "I'll get up." "Oh, hell, no, I've done it already." He was swishing tea-leaves round, he would dump them expertly on a bit of newspaper, spread open on the carpet, and rinse out the tea-pot behind the Spanish screen with fresh water from the wash-stand jug, before he poured the preliminary boiling water in the brown pot. Then he would rinse that out again, measure in the tea. Chinaman, is that it? Was he a Chinaman? Was he Aladdin, was the teapot the magic lamp? There was some-thing of that in this, but really her intuitions were sub-merged, so deeply submerged that when they flowed over her (tide-wave) as now, the moment, the mood, they were of a depth of subconscious being for which there were no words. Bliss. Stepping on the blue square of carpet, before the low double-couch, their bed, she had pulled away from the endangering emotional paralysis. Sheets, a bed, a tomb. But walking for the first time, taking the first steps in her life, upright on her feet for the first time alone, or for the first time standing after death (daughter, I say unto thee), she faced the author of this her momentary psychic being, her lover, her husband. It was like that, in these moments. She touched paradise.

He too. But he did not have to think of that. He was going away to-morrow. To-day? He slapped down the tea-pot, as if he had scorched his fingers. "Look at it—I forgot it." "It?" She was walking normally, naturally, she was walking out of the mood (paradise) toward the table; she was coming-to from drowning; she was waking out of aether. "Oh, the—time—" she looked at the thing he was looking at; his service wrist-watch was spread flat with its leather strap on the table. Its disc was covered with round woven wire, like a tiny basket, bottom side up, or a fencer's mask. Time in prison, that time. It ticked merrily away, inside its little steel cage.

"I can actually hear it ticking." She had to say some-thing. For she couldn't do this again, she couldn't do this again, she couldn't do this again.

"Hullo, what's happened to it?"
"Oh, it just went on ticking. They do."
She peered through the fencer's mask into the bird-cage, she took up the watch, she shook it. "Maybe it's stopped."
"Stopped?"
"I mean, maybe it stopped at tea-time." She held it to her ear. True, she had heard its insistent insect tick-tick. The room was so quiet. Standing, she had heard above a table the voice of time on a table, the little voice that said,

"It's time, it's time." The little demon or devil or daemon was alive. She knew of course that it hadn't stopped at tea-time.

"Well, it's tea-time, anyhow."

"Any time is tea-time," she said.

"I'll wash those cups." Cups were scattered on the table and some rose-leaves. They had been out for dinner.

"Why wash them? We haven't got foot-and-mouth disease." He rinsed two cups behind the Spanish screen however, while she stood there. She was coming back but she had to do little things to stay here. She had to act; in action, stage-business, she over-acted, "Stockings, I'm cold." She drew stockings up under her nightdress; will they stay up? She found a woolly sweater, dragged on her out-door coat that she had left, flung over one of the small upright chairs by the book-case.

"Let's have those eggs."

"Eggs?"

"Eggs—"

"But what will you have for breakfast? But look at the blighter." She went back to the table. She looked at the living little daemon, though she knew what the hands marked. "It's half-past four, it's getting on for five. Ho—breakfast."

Breakfast. Break fast. They would break their fast. "Boiled? Fried? Scrambled?"

"Oh, anything. The easiest. I'd better put on my clothes" (she had to say something), "get dressed. I'm coming with you."

"You're not—this time—Anthea."

He called her Anthea. It was Julie, Judy, Judy-bird, or Julie-bird. Anthea. He said it again. His eyes had a vague look, what was he looking at, she wondered. He must not go-off like that, his eyes must stay-put, stay normal, fixed on this room.

He must not look out across a sheet of slate-cold water, to another continent, to France.

"Every cigarette. This one—" but she couldn't finish what she started to say. Surely they were too tired, surely they were worn out, surely it was impossible for him to cover her mouth with kisses.

"This one," he said, "this one," he said, "this one."

"You'll put out my cigarette."

"Is that all you care? This one," he repeated. His hand clutched at her shoulder through the out-door coat, through the woolly stuff of the pullover, through the thin stuff of the nightdress underneath it.

"This one and this one," he said. One hand wavered, held on to the torch burning; fingers tightened round the fresh-lit cigarette. She was holding on to something, the small spark of fire, the smouldering at the end of an incense stick, her cigarette.

"And this one—" she assembled what might have been herself, not so much to push him off, as to hold herself to-gether.

It was five o'clock, it would soon be six, it was morning, it would soon be day. "And this—and this—" he said, but his face was the same, the somewhat coarsened, heavy, blunt face, the wide eyes that were still somewhat vague for all the present intensity of the moment. The same shoulders—and her other hand, protesting like a leaf of Vallombrosa, as he called it, found itself resting on the stuff of the camel-hair coat that was the same colour, if you came to think of it, as the khaki tunic that now, soon, he would put on. There was all the difference. Soon, he would be assembled, off, *bid me to love. Bid me to die. Loved I not honour more.* But that was the catch, that was what was the matter. It would have been reasonably easy, if they had wholly believed in it, to play at seventeenth-century gallantry, or to play Electra and the dead. Death? It was not possible. He was going to say it. He did say it. "Remember if I don't come back or if I do come back and anything happens (if anything gets between us), remember this was this, and this is always." Always? It was a long time.

The ghost, whatever it was, was not dead. Ghosts don't, of course, die. That was it. It had been, even in the beginning, a sort of emanation. Something they had between them. Its moments were prolonged, would last a day, a day and a night. The thing between them, that they conjured up together, would be a flash-light through a wall. And this side was this reality, this table, this chair, three long windows with double blue curtains (I hemmed them myself) just touching the floor. Behind the blue curtains were the old-fashioned, inward-opening inside-shutters with the iron bolts. The bolts were drawn. Back of the three curtains were three bolted doors, they opened out on an iron balcony that looked over a town square. There were three doors; they opened out into other rooms, other vistas. She did not think this.

Her eyes, rather, took in the details of the room itself, this table, these two cups and the half-dozen other cups, shoved to one side by the heap of papers and a pile of books and the ash-trays. There must have been a party. Her mind concentrated, focused on tea-time, this afternoon, or yesterday. Then she brushed aside the memory of this room full, as it always was at tea-time, it seemed now, with people. "We want to see Rafe." "He'll be back again soon." "Don't forget to let us know," and they would finally be pushed down steps, out of the front door with the old-fashioned Regency fanlight. Well, that's over.

She always felt he wanted to see people, lighted up, laughing with lots of people. She brushed off the memory of people. She had asked people. She had kept in touch during his absence. She wondered if she could ever manage it again.

"All those cups—"

"Don't worry, I'll wash them up before—before I go."

"I don't mean that. I meant—us—together—here—no one."

But it was better to have people, Morgan laughing, Morgan le Fay, of course, they had to call her. Ivan, before he went to Petrograd. The boy in the Italian cape. Who was he? Half Italian on the way to Rome, that last time. Captain Ned Trent who had been in the Boer War, was now an Irish rebel. Morgan again. And Morgan. "How did you think Morgan was looking this time?" But don't let's talk of Morgan. Why Morgan? It was at her house, I met Rafe.

She did not ask the question, did not ask any questions.

She could ask a question, chatter about the people who had been here at tea-time, but she knew now it was too late. The mood, maybe for the last time, was on them.

But she knew that was not true, for she could invoke the mood at any time, over a tea-cup with a cigarette, any time after he left. She had lived with him, absent, so intensely. He would be almost nearer, once he had gone, than he was now. But he hadn't gone yet.

She must hold the thing; like a tight-rope walker, she must move tip-toe across an infinitely narrow thread, a strand, the rope, the umbilical cord, the silver-cord that bound them to that past. The past had been blasted to hell, you might say; already, in 1917, the past was gone. It had been blasted and blighted, the old order was dead, was dying, was being bombed to bits, was no more. But that was not true. Reality lived in the minds of those who had lived before that August. They had lived then. They had had that year in Italy, before the war, almost a year of married life in England after. Two years. One married year in England and the time together, before that, in Paris, in Rome. In Capri, Verona, Venice.

Words that she did not speak held old cities together; on this fine strand, this silver-cord, Venice was a bright glass-bead, certainly a translucent emerald-green, a thing in itself, in itself worth all the misery of the past two years. 1914. Then 1915 and her death, or rather the death of her child. Three weeks in that ghastly nursing-home and then coming back to the same Rafe. Herself different. How could

she blithely face what he called love, with that prospect
looming ahead and the matron, in her harsh voice, laying
a curse on whatever might then have been, "You know you
must not have another baby until after the war is over."
Meaning in her language, you must keep away from your
husband, keep him away from you. When he was all she
had, was country, family, friends. Well—that anyway. And
roses on her pillow and "Darling, you have come back."

Roses?

There were roses on the table now, petals fell on tea-
cups. People had been in, then. She could chat about peo-
ple, Morgan—the boy in the Italian cape—that was it. That
brought back visibly (on a thread) beads that were tiny
cities, or tiny cities were in her hand like the symbolic cities
in the folds of a Pope's robe, painted on a triptych. "We're
painted on a triptych."

"What did you say, Julie?"

"I was thinking of Italy—"

"Open my heart and you will see—"

"Yes—"

"—graved inside of it," he chanted in mock unction,
"Italy," but he didn't dare think, himself did not dare
realize how frail the cord was, how heavy the memories
strung along the frail spider-web of a silver-cord that might
so soon be broken.

"Or ever the pitcher—"

Oh, God, had she said that? No, just breathed it. He
had been so unhappy when she had quoted, *ten thousand
shall fall*. "Well," said Rafe Ashton, "over the top."

He had said that before. She knew the answer to that.

"I'm coming with you."

"No," he said, "no."

She sorted out her clothes, shook out her garter-belt. "Stop," he said.

He snatched the web of elastic and silk from her. It was a pretty belt, she had made it for this, salvaged the elastic straps from an old pair, sewed on the old buttons. He flung the silk and faded elastic with the tight sewed-on buttons, that fastened at the back, across the room.

"You're not going out in this fog."

"How do you know it is fog?"

"Simpleton—it's dark."

"Not any darker, if you come to think of it, than it was at the same time, the last time on the clock. I mean at six or seven last night—"

"Last night was—last night—"

It meant nothing. She retrieved the garter-belt. Then her knees gave. She sank down on the other little upright chair, the other side of the book-case. There were two of these gilt chairs with the faded elegant silk and the slightly dimmed gilt. They were Miss Ames' chairs, along with the Spanish screen which she had asked them if they would mind keeping on, in the room.

Half of their things from the last flat in Hampstead were stacked with some of the books and two-thirds of the kitchen things and china, in the packing-cases in the basement. This was their bed. She ran over the furniture, inventory. She looked up. He was strapping on his Sam Browne. He stepped to the knapsack, drew it toward him, then dragged it to the bed. He sat clothed now, a British officer on leave, on the edge of the bed. He tightened the fastenings of the knapsack and then suddenly unfastened them. He was looking for something. Then he strapped on his watch. Then he unstrapped his watch. "Come here."

She got up from the ridiculous gilt chair, like an odd lost chair from fifty or a hundred chairs, the sort people hire to fill drawing-rooms for a wedding. The gilt chair had become fifty gilt chairs, though she did not turn to look at it, nor to look at the other matching it, where she had neatly folded her clothes last night. The habit of a life-time. The chairs were multiplied; now she saw the table piled on top of the table piled on top of the table. The room was swaying, air-raid fashion, though the ceiling had not come down. Then she noticed that it was very quiet. So this is not an air-raid. She trailed across the floor, trailing her out-door coat in her hand; busy now with the other hand, she fumbled to pull at her pullover, to pull it over her head. He pulled it off, snatched the coat from her, pushed her back on the bed, drew the bedclothes over her, tucked the grey out-door coat around her.

He sat on the edge of the bed and again fumbled in the knapsack, "I want you to keep something for me, something very precious. Promise."

"Yes," she said. "I promise."

He laid a bundle of letters on the top of the coat, pulled over her.

"What's this?"

"It's something very precious, the last batch of letters that you sent me. I almost took them back again."

"I'll send others to you."

"I know—you'll—send—others—to—me—" His head was bent over the knapsack. The back of his head was smooth. His shoulders were British officer, out of a tailor's window. Did tailors have officers in windows? His sleeve had a bit of trimming, not much. She put out her hand to touch it. The back of her hand brushed something on the bed-spread. She turned her hand and her fingers felt metal.

"Why, it's your watch. You're forgetting your watch."

She held the leather strap, pushed back the covers, sat up with her bare arms exposed. He was right, it was cold. I really must go with him. He had found his hat now. He was running his fingers over the backs of the books. He flung his hat down. Now he adjusted the straps over his shoulders, looked round the room.

"Your watch," she was holding it out to him, with the leather strap.

He took the strap from her. He sat down on the bed beside her. She pushed back the khaki sleeve with the little strip of trimming, she ran her fingers round his firm wrist. She made a bracelet of both her hands. She tightened the grasp. Then she reached out for the strap. "Let me put it on." But he pushed her aside, he pushed her away, he looked at the watch.

"Over the top," he said. He had said that before. "Poor stuff, Fritz," he said. Then he took her hand in his hand, he held the strap around it. "It's too big," he said, he pulled the strap to its last leather eyelet, then he got up. He fumbled on the table, he slapped a pocket, he was prodding at the strap with a penknife.

"What's wrong?"

"Your wrist," he said, "I told you it was too thin." He was prodding at the strap.

"You'll spoil it."

"It?" His head was bent, his shoulders were the shoulders of a British officer on leave. He was going away. Don't think about the shoulders. Now he took her hand roughly. "Fingers," he said, "too thin. Good for nothing—good for poetry." Now he kissed her fingers, but what was all this? People don't cry. We don't.

"It's time you went. Oh, I did want to go with you, if you'll only let me get up, it's not too late, I can yet go with you."

But he fastened the leather round her wrist, he tightened it with a hard twist, he bent over her hand, secured the strap in the fresh-cut eye-hole. "It fits now," he said.

"Yes," she said, tugging at the strap to pull off the officer's wrist-watch that had been last time in Loos, Lenz? Where was it? Where is this? I can't see anything.

He took both hands in his. Two hands in his.

"I don't want it, damn it," he said. "I'm leaving it with you, to give you some idea—" what was he saying? Now there was nothing but the rough khaki under her throat. Her chin brushed buttons, her thin-clad chest felt buttons, he was holding her too tight. She didn't say anything. Then she said,

"Go away, go away, or it will be too late."

"Too late," he said, "it's damn near too late—and if—"

"Don't say it," she said. "Don't say anything."

"Just this," he said, "wear this for me, one out of suits

with fortune, who would give more—who would give more
—but that—"

She was crying on the pillow. He didn't see me crying.
She heard the front door thud, like the front door thudded
when there was a thick fog.

III

Why did he give me his watch? The watch went on ticking. He had shut this door so quietly that she did not know he had gone, though she knew he had gone. She knew he had gone when the front door thudded; he has gone. This has happened before. Would it always go on happening? That time in Corfe Castle when she reminded him that love is stronger than death. Was it? Why yes. She had been going on living with death and she was alive. She was stronger. But love? Everything that happened had happened so quickly. But was two years, was three, quick? It was a long time. Time. It went on ticking.

Now she knew why it was alive, its hands were phosphorescent. Her eyes opened, fastened on the green arrows, of course he had switched off the light as he stood by the door. Why did he have to do that? Leaving her an invalid in a bed with the light switched off; now go to sleep. Her face was cracked where salt had left stripes down her face. Stripes? His first. She had pay. But she sent it back to him. She had her allowance from America to live on, and she

sent back her separation allowance so that he and some of
the other Tommies (before he had his commission) would
have the price of coffee or beer or whatever it was they got
in those dug-out *estaminets*, where they crowded in the rain.
Was it always raining?

Her heart simply wasn't there. It was elevated, lifted;
in bed, she felt that light-headedness that meant she was
free. Why, of course, she didn't care. Why should she? She
would be alone now to recover from this last leave, till the
next leave, if there was a next leave. He was dead already,
already he had died a half-dozen times, he was always dying.

"I won't come back," he had said the last time but he
came back. This time? Time? Yes, that was it. She said to
herself, it's alive, chirping. It was that little cricket in a
basket they had bought on May-day in Florence and let
loose. The Florentines plaited grass into little baskets and
caught crickets or grasshoppers; it was out of Theocritus,
he said. They bought a little basket and emptied the some-
what doped-looking insect into a tub of carnations, outside
the café with striped awnings opposite the Baptistry. Trams
jangled past, very noisy. The carnations were wine-colour,
sops-in-wine he called them. Sops-in-wine? Sop to Cer-
berus. This was.

He had given her something, as if for the last time. It
was always the last time. Well, let it be the last time. She
did not think of Morgan and her flowered extravagance, the
mauve chemise she had slept in with me, in this bed. "Only
let me stay, I'll sleep on the floor," said Morgan. So they
said, "But no, Rafe will sleep on the cot behind the screen;
you stay." It was one of Morgan's many complications, she
had to spend the rest of the night somewhere. It did not

seem in any way perverse or wrong, it was just Morgan. They helped her out, that time, gave her breakfast, the three of them in this room. But can this go on? It would have been better if Morgan had slept with him in this bed, not with me. Would it?

"Of course you'll tell Stephen that I spent the whole night with you—if—or anybody—I mean, no one is likely to ask—but—"

"Of course," they said.

The peculiar honk-honk of the new taxis, the lop-lop of the old fiacres, the smell of petrol. There were those same pinks, but white clusters, rained on from a French water-pot that he kept hidden under the bunches, trois sous la botte. They had compared those later May Italian pinks with the summer pinks in Paris. The Italian ones were growing in a tub, very hot sun and the awning cast very black shadow. The shadow of the Duomo moved across the square, as they sat over raspberries. Now the scent of petrol was French petrol, and the kiosks made them laugh, like those ubiquitous urinoirs, "Go in one just for fun, what can it be like inside?" "But you can see the whole show from the outside," he said. Paris. The sticky asphalt was soft to their feet. They found the Louvre was closed. It's always closed on Monday. They had forgotten that. They trailed across the bridge and walked to the Cluny Museum, where there were Gothic fragments, stuck up against the wall. She didn't want to sketch Gothic fragments, but it was cool there. They compared their sketch-books, his drawings were niggling and tight, hers better conceived but vague in outline. His were squat and too tight. They completed each other, even in their crude sketches; "Between us we might make an artist," he said.

It was raining, rain beat against the high window, rain in a stage-set. It was a stage-set. Corfe could not be true. The castle loomed out of mist, when finally they decided they must get a breath of air. They couldn't stick upstairs in that tiny room all day. He was going back to France. France? But France was asphalt melting under a down-trodden, scuffed heel, "I ought to get these mended." They walked back to the *Île de France* and sat in the shade on the cobble-stones by the river and she started to sketch one of the heads that ornamented the bridge, while he scribbled on the back of an old envelope.

"Come and kiss me, pretty sweeting, journeys end in lovers meeting," he remarked conversationally to a barge that was nosing its way along the island. The river, for river water, was clear enough, it was setting up a little sputter, it crept along the edge of the stones, a rope trailed with a soft hiss and spit of water. The boat passed.

The sun was getting round the bridge, it was too bright in her eyes. She was only blocking in the stone-face that had no intrinsic value, like a plaster-cast face of faun or satyr in a drawing-school. She blocked round it, it gave her a sense of continuity, it gave her her own proportion, placed her in the centre of a circle, which she measured, mock-profes-sionally, with a pencil held before her. When she squinted at the pencil, she was not so much seeing the thing she was about to block in roughly, as making a circle, with a com-pass, for herself to stay in. There was so much around them.

"What are you drawing, Julie?"

"Well, I wasn't exactly, it gives one a sort of vantage point—to get into the circle—I mean—"

"You always get cryptic when it's time for your cup of tea at tea-time, though why you want that blasted stuff in this city of the vintages—" he trailed off.

Vintages, she thought, he's probably thinking out a rhyme for vintages, it doesn't work, he'll have to go back and end his line with grapes though we went all over those, apes, japes, rapes—though that isn't any too good either unless he's writing something bawdy.

"Are you writing something bawdy?"

"Wilt thou yet take all, Galilean?" he questioned. He answered, "But this thou shalt not take." He screwed the addressed envelope with the English stamp into a cone and contradictorily aimed it toward the water. The cone swirled backward and untwisted and the envelope unfolded at her feet.

She smoothed out the crumpled paper. "*Season of mists and mellow fruitfulness,*" she read. "But that's Shelley," she said for the pleasure of hearing him say, "it's Keats," the sort of thing one did say, but he didn't say it.

Now she said, "Why can't you write your own poetry?" trying not to wonder who addressed the envelope. "Why can't you?"

"It's too hot," he said.

What was he thinking of when he wrote *season of mists?* London?

"Well—what—" she came back, she had stacked the dishes on the wash-stand behind the screen.

He looked up from his book. "Why—" he said—
"why—"

He wasn't there at all. It was the thing that frightened
her, that made her say, "This can't go on, I must have peo-
ple in all the time, it can't go on." Why did he start reading
the *Madrigals*? Why did he stop reading? He's looking for
another book—the *Hesperides*? He's wondering. He's not
here. No, he wasn't there. It was almost better when she
was alone.

All of the *Hesperides* was there, nearer than the table,
than the mantelpiece; the assortment of books, his pipes,
tobacco bowl, everything was seen through the clear pattern
of the projected images; the spike of an orange-tree with
fruit and blossom and the scent of the blossom was nearer
than this was. But his eyes must not stare out.

"Oh, how did you think—I mean what did you think—"
how was she to speak to him, she wanted to clap her hands,
say "Wake-up, wake-up," but what would she wake him up
to?

Now the watch weighed her wrist to her chest, weighed
a weight on her chest. The watch was a stone weighing her
there.

She lifted her wrist under the bed-covers, she let it fall
back. She clenched her cold fingers under the bed-covers.
The wrist-watch was a stone, scarab weighing her to this bed.

It was not always such a happy bed. Witness to—to—she
could not think of happiness, remembering one night
(two? three nights ago?) when he had muttered inco-

herently of "that's the stuff" and some horses that got
caught in their traces or reins and something that happened
to someone pulling on the reins, and then something that
had happened to the horses. Maybe he was making it up,
and lying tense and cold beside him she thought that it
might be better for him to go on; she did not know if he
were awake or asleep. She did not know whether it was
better to pretend to be there, to fling arms about a stranger.
Now she wondered if he were making it up or was he dream-
ing? Did he want to make this up, to ruin what she had so
carefully preserved, the fact of this room, the continuity of
this bed, the presence of herself, the same self beside him?
No, he was not making it up.

Beauty is truth, truth beauty. But could this truth be
beautiful? Maybe it was. They had shouted of honour and
sacrifice for two years, three years now. This was winter or
early spring but seasons revolved around horrors until one
was numb and the posters that screamed at one at street-
corners had no more reality, not as much, as the remem-
bered Flemish gallery of the Louvre and the abstract-painted
horror of a flayed saint—they were past feeling anything;
she was. He was right, then, maybe, when he said "You
don't feel anything."

It might be seven or eight, but no, not as late as that be-
cause there would be the running of feet, the munition girls
from the top floor going to work. There had been, there
must have been, the scrape of the milk bottles on the stone
slab of the Regency doorway, but maybe she was asleep;

anyhow she didn't always hear the boy set down the bottles. Martha's husband had lately been reported lost, swept off a raft in a river, Mesopotamia (Mespot, Rafe called it).

Things like that were so utterly fantastic, Martha would set the bottle down outside her door; she opened the front door, collected the bottles and delivered them at the several landings. Maybe the milk bottle was there, anyhow she would have to get up because Martha barged in to "do" for her, on the way upstairs, although lately she had brushed her away, they had "done" for themselves, there was so little time, they were so seldom alone. This morning would be the worst, for Martha would commiserate; Julia would be forced to listen to a story again that was Robinson Crusoe fantasy, a raft in a river. Mespot, out of the Bible, Euphrates? Should she get up?

She tugged at the strap of the wrist-watch. The catch was firm, fastened into the little new eyelet that he had made, now only such a short time ago, with the pen-knife on the table or a pen-knife (which?) that he had salvaged from his pocket. No, it was the one on the table. She saw the glint of the worn mother-of-pearl handle. The knife had one largish blade, notched, and a small needle-like blade. It must have been the small blade.

She saw that the little sharp blade was still left open, where he had left it on the table. Had it been opened? Why had he not clasped it, why hadn't he shut the little blade automatically, as one does a pen-knife?

The room was cold, but a little heady, stuffy with their cigarettes. It was really, when you come to think of it, a short time ago, their breakfast really. But she must get up.

She lifted the watch and saw the aluminium green-pale face in the just-visible grey infiltration of light from over the tops of the curtains and through the crack in the shutter, opposite her bed. It was jewel-green, the little hands had moved, it was after eight. The munitions workers must have gone out. Now she remembered that it was Sunday and, thank God, after all, Martha would not come in.

Herself, she could stay here but the cold lead of her forehead, the rather heavier lead of the back of her head, were filled with an aura of slight burning. Her mind had been snuffed out, for an hour; they had not really slept last night. This short sleep was one of those asbestos curtains that bangs down; it had not quite done its job. The blaze and flame of chemicals was in the room, in the back of her head, her forehead was cooler. She might manage it somehow that the whole head calmed down and the muddle of poisonous gas and flayed carcasses be dispersed somehow. It was actually a taste in her lungs, though while he was here, she had not recognised it, said it was some sort of vague idea, but she knew it was true. He had breathed a taint of poison-gas in her lungs, the first time he kissed her. He had coughed a little but then she said, "It's the room, we should open the windows, it's stuffy in here." She said, "We're smoking too much."

She dragged upright, flung her feet out of the bed. She stood on the carpet, felt for bedroom slippers. Walked to a chair, dragged his camel-hair dressing-gown about her, fastened it with the cord. It was warmer than her own. She walked to the window by the book-case and unlatched a shutter, let it sag open just a wide crack so that she could see to find the matches. She found matches, lit the gas, filled the tea-kettle with fresh water from the jug—thank God there's still enough left. She turned down the flame that was wasting itself in a halo round the outside of the small kettle. She washed out a cup.

In a moment something would come right, even in this room. Even in this room, the old charm, even early on a war-Sunday morning in a war-ridden city, in a city of—of—*mist and mellow fruitfulness*. Well, yes it had been that, anyway, everything came to me here, here I had everything. How could anyone imagine that I would go back to America? Here I found—found— There was the packet of letters on the floor where they had slipped when she jerked out of the bed. His name and no stamp. "Remember, you always forget, you need not waste stamps on letters out here."

Out there? The train would be moving off, she was spared the horror of that. She had seen so many trains in, off, inevitably running into rows of returned invalids, and what am I doing? What am I doing? She flicked the bit of string off the bundle of letters, spread them fan-wise on the table, knew that she couldn't bear to read them. Eight, ten, twelve, fourteen—I will write him to-day.

What was it that happened? It was as definite as putting on a dress, as pulling up stockings, as fastening the garter-belt and tightening the stocking-web into the rubber-lined garter-catches, four. Automatically, you did these things, without thinking. A form of automatic mood flowed over her with the second cup of tea, it would embrace her, enfold her with the first puff of the cigarette, her morning cigarette, after the cup of tea. She was a creature of habits, she moved in a room to a sort of precise rhythm, the garter-belt, the stockings were attributes of a dance, they were attributes. The pot of tea, the match-box, the cigarette. There are only three left. I must get some more.

She shook out the three cigarettes on the table, they lay there in a formation, she would read the formation, like reading tea-leaves, or like reading a message in the pattern made by the fallen rose-leaves on the table. The roses are all but faded. She struck a match and she drew in a deep breath and the drug, the anodine, was about to free her. Flicking out the match, she carefully placed it in the agate ash-tray that held the stubbed-out ends of an orgy of cigarette smoking yesterday, last night; she saw that the patch of light, left by the swung-back shutter, was blocked in, in stronger outline. It was a white door of light in a dim room that smelt of tea-leaves, of half-wilted roses, of this fresh cigarette and last night's. I suppose I should open the window, she thought.

She breathed in this sort of fug (his word) which was, after all, the incense of last night's burning. Into her lungs, appositely, she drew the very pattern in the air, their words made. She seemed to eat the very air, what was it Lett Barnes said in the old days when he first came to London? Something about duck-eggs, yes, he had bought duck-eggs because they were bigger and even the difference in the size of eggs had then made a difference. He was her first poet. He had said that starvation or near-starvation, practised systematically, would produce the same effect as dope.

He said, "I don't recommend it," looking rather stark, in that way he had of looking, like a somewhat Dakota Dante.

He had met something face to face here, but that wasn't a war. Add to the "systematic starvation," the constant flayed nerves and the constant brutality of the present and you get something even—even—finer was not the word to describe it. She was walking on a very, very thin wire; she was wandering like a dope-fiend in a not-known dimension. This she knew certainly. A sense of all-pervading comfort. The hollow of the groins or loins almost felt the shape of the curious bottle-necked digestive objects in it. Purified. Exactly, they practised these things in temples, Yogi, Tibet, Eleusinian Mysteries, but here they got that sort of psychic initiation all the same, every day. It had gone on too long.

But just now, it was as if she had reached some definite turning-point, or some point where, if she did not keep her balance, she would fall off. The last straw. Not yet. A matchstick placed carefully on the edge of an agate ash-tray that was filled with stubbed-out ends of yesterday's, of last night's cigarettes was not the last straw. Not to-day, anyway. To-day she would relate to yesterday and by a subtle and valiant trick of léger-de-main, to to-morrow. The thread binding past and present was not broken, would not yet break. She was living along a thin wire, or thin living web, bound actually to someone in a train, with a great turn-up collar. He would be sleeping in a corner. Across the fine thread ran some sort of aura, as if she actually and consistently fed from him, in her middle. As if he (so he said) was kept alive, just by the fact of her being here in London, by the letters that she sent him.

Dear Rafe,
    There's nothing to write about because you've only just gone. I got up and the letters fell out on the floor. They're here on the table. I won't read them. I

know that what I am writing is written in all those, and then, maybe, I won't write. I've got on your dressing-gown. The third window by the book-case is letting in enough light to see by, to see this by. Really, I'm writing in the dark for if I open my mind's eye, I shall see things as—impossible. You know. I mean, this eye is that inward eye (God help us all) which is the bliss of solitude.

Those Wordsworth daffodils, they seem cold and non-conformist, they're not the daffodils we weep to see. Or daffodils that come before the swallow. And take the winds of March. And take the Ides of March . . .

She had finished the page. She began another. What I write really isn't anything but I'm sure the mood comes through; he says it does and anyhow, he likes me to write about Italy—

sing frost sing indefinite cold isles sing every cold sweet stinging grain of white hail and sing all formed and formative deep-sown earth-grains each separate sing for the new-time come and out of the old war-wreck and the piled heap of iron repair its share ploughshare turn old mould cast out bones white coral eaten so white that every man will turn and see white coral island of bones—

She tore this up. It was Shakespeare making her think of England, full fathom five . . . are coral made.
She went on with the letter.

I started a sort of poem. It was the idea of March. Writing letters to you and writing poetry go along in the same sort of groove, I mean when I get into the mood of writing a letter, I feel I can rush headlong down the proverbial cliff. If I glean anything worth typing out, I'll send it and please remember that any scraps on old envelopes must wing back here—doves? Turtle. That verse, the voice of the turtle is heard in the land always worried me, but it was the turtle-dove, why didn't they say so? He feedeth among the lilies. Do you remember those somewhat filthy frogs at Sirmione?

Well, where will you be now with your overcoat collar turned up, asleep? Or have you fumbled in your fabulous old kit-bag for your pipe yet?

Well, we should weep to see you haste away so soon, but I'm so in-grown and comfortable at this moment, my first cigarette, these books, that I can't even cry about your going. Because you're coming back so soon. Love, Anthea.

IV

Everything had to fall to pieces sooner or later; well, why not sooner? Then, at least, you get it over, face the worst, know. She had already faced the worst inwardly; not actually facing the actual facts, but resounding to them, as it were, or refracted back from them, reflected when things became impossible, and anyhow, however, come to grips with him? His "I won't come back next time" destroyed all possibility of contact.

You could not argue. His moods were more violent. He was not really the young officer on leave; that was not Rafe. Then if that was not Rafe, well, let it be not-Rafe; the disintegrating factor was the glance, the look, the throwing aside of the uniform and the turn of the head, a stranger standing over by the book-shelf, *was* Rafe Ashton. That is my husband, that is the man I married. The stranger became singularly strange, his language, his voice, the thing he brought into the room. Well, can you blame him? He was colourating to what he was, who is Julia Ashton to deny that?

Julia Ashton is the last person in the world to minimise

the thing he goes through. Back and forth from France—
now he is actually enjoying it. Now he likes it. But I can not
serve God and Mammon, not serve poet and hearty over-
sexed ("we have them on the run") young officer on leave.
I love you, Rafe, but stay away, don't come back; don't, for
God's sake, take that book now off the shelf, don't turn now
and be Rafe; stay away, don't mangle my emotions any
more.

I spared you what I went through, you do not spare me. I
did not tell you; my agony in the Garden had no words.

Don't go on, for I can not tell you, what happened two
years ago, what happened two and a half years ago; this is
late summer, early autumn 1917. Have you been back be-
tween this leave, and the one in which you strapped your
watch to my wrist? I can't get it straight. Yes—there must
have been the usual parties, a little more than usual, for
Bella Carter's here, has been here now all summer and this
is late summer or early autumn, and yes, she was here at
some of the parties last time. So there was an intermediate
leave, when you hadn't quite gone, when you read "O
daffodils" again and "Bid me to live." Then, there was the
going away and now this. Now this. Now this.

This time, you are all but submerged, is there any use
any longer sweating agony in a Garden? I had my cruci-
fixion. I can't go back, step over my own corpse and sweat
blood, now that you are what you are. If you let it alone, if
you just managed to be one person, the young officer, rather
hearty and too loud, why, then that would be that. I can not
hold the poet to what he had and live, and surely he loved
me. Maybe, I am the snag.

It couldn't be a worse muddle. There he stood. She noted the season by the great sheaf of tawny red and copper-red chrysanthemums on the table. This was the season—of—of mellow fruitfulness. A great, over-sexed officer on leave, who had thrown off his tunic, is mellow fruitfulness. His body was harder, he was as they say well set-up, his head was bronze on the less bronze shoulders, he was perfectly proportioned, a little heavy but a late-Roman, rather than Greek image, that walked about a room, himself with no clothes on.

A bronze late-Roman image had got out of the wrong department in the Louvre or the British Museum, something that moved and talked, like the picture of the Roman soldier in the Judgment of Solomon in their child's illustrated Bible spread open on the floor. She did not actually put this two and two together. Though obviously something was being severed, was being cut in half. Already Bella had begun insistence, "He can't have it both ways," and "You tyrannize his spirit." Already the thing was cut in half, not so neatly, Siamese-twin mangled tentacles still bound Rafe-Julia together. His "Bella is a star-performer" was the remark of a stranger, of someone friendly but of another world, another dimension, telling her in a friendly manner that Bella was a star-performer.

All that. So far, so good. If he, if she had just left it at that, if they had had the decency to move out of this house, to leave me alone. But decency? Was she decent? A decent wife does not permit this—this— But that wife, cut in half (all wives are now), meets a stranger, hears strange words from a strange throat and then hears, "I lived till I got back,

I knew you'd remember to leave the *Madrigals* where I'd find them."

Then in the last air-raid when the books had fallen out of the tilted shelf, like books in a play depicting a scene in an earthquake, he had kicked the books across the floor, playing football with them, really showing off for Bella and the other wild people at the party. But who was she to stand out, primly, to collect books, to put them back on a shelf that was tilted like the wall of a ship sinking at sea? Who was she to bar the shutters, to sweep up the broken glass? Leave broken glass and sing "It's a long, long way" and agree that someone might "wangle" something at the pub in Theobalds Road, if they went quickly. It was Rafe and Bella who went.

He came back from Theobalds Road; he said, "She flung her arms round me in the Square," and speaking, as if from outside, like someone in a play, Julia heard Julia speaking, "Well, what? I mean, what are you and she going to do about it?" It was better to know. She knew.

Then he left, leaving the scattered books and the broken windows and the rest of the admittedly exaggerated and disproportionate nonsense for her to deal with.

"Grey-eyed goddess," Ivan had called her. Then "grey-eyed goddess," Ivan had written, "I hear from Bella Carter, she has had to leave Paris, would you keep an eye on her, we want to be together when I get back from Petrograd." And "grey-eyed goddess, you are the only woman in the world of whom I could ask this. She's run wild. I want to look after her when I get back from Petrograd." So this was the Bella that Ivan had left with her, leaving it to her to see that Bella did not get too lonely, that Bella did not run too wild, "let her talk to you. I know that you can help her."

Help Bella Carter?

Well—yes—no—I mean, let Bella Carter help me. I can not go on with this. At nobody's instigation, Bella flung her arms round Rafe in the garden on the way home from the pub in Theobalds Road where they went to "wangle" something for the dregs of what was left of that party, after the air-raid when the books fell out on the floor and the windows sagged inward, dropping tinkling glass on the floor, like a ship floundering in a too-heavy sea.

Now the room was still. The window-panes had been put back. The book-shelf stood steady. The books, more or less irregularly set up, were yet books on a book-shelf. The bronze late-Roman had tied a rope round a camel-hair dressing-gown and by that familiar gesture was no longer the easy problem, "Well, you and Bella must work that out between you." This creature was familiar, he was turning toward the mantelpiece to look for a pipe, he was Rafe Ashton, my husband.

Fighting not so much a losing as a lost-battle, she went on. It could not go on. Even now his "I won't come back, you might allow me a little fun" was someone else speaking. It was not Rafe speaking. The two did not speak consecutive lines, the dividing sword had not yet done its work. (Would it ever?) This *persona grata* with the bronze head emerging from the familiar camel-hair dressing-gown, the Saint Anthony's robe with its monk-rope tied in a knot round those loins, was not sufficiently separated to make it sane. His very detachment toward Bella was part of the crazy-quilt, it was patch-work. There was no going straight on, holding on, planning the frugal festivals, asking people in now. Yet this was the same room. The window-panes had been smashed, the books had fallen out on the floor, but it was the same house.

It is true that Bella Carter was upstairs in Ivan's little bedroom. But Bella was part of a play, she had her entrances, she had her exits. How blame Bella? There was no blame anywhere. Or if there was blame, it was Julia's; she was holding on to something that had been smashed to hell. Why had she not just let it all go? Two years, three years, Paris, the Louvre. All those things were stacked in cellars, the galleries would be empty. Everybody was waiting for everything to be smashed. Why pretend that life could possibly be the same, ever? Why pretend, here in this room, in this house, that this was her room, this is my bed. Nothing belonged to anybody, the room was common-room, birds of passage roosted and rooted and parties certainly had smashed what lines had been left in the air by the casual reading of *Hesperides*—was it? Words had made a pattern, delicate yet firm, clear etched as the little wire cage on the face of the watch he gave her. The watch was the same watch, but time was different. Months, days were smashed. There was no continuity. She had given up pretending.

"What's this?" he said.

"That?" She was waiting for him to say something in keeping with this whole mad show. He should say, "Bella is waiting for me upstairs, Bella is a star-performer, Bella understands these things, I'm going up to Bella."

"Old Rico," he said, "what's dam' old Frederico writing?"

"Read it," she said.

Dear Julia,
There is no use trying to believe that all this war really exists. It really doesn't matter. We must go on. I know that Rafe will come back. Your frozen altars mean something, but I don't like the second half of the Orpheus sequence as well as the first. Stick to the woman speaking. How can you know what Orpheus feels? It's your part to be woman, the woman vibration, Eurydice should be enough. You can't deal with both. If you go on—

"Go on, what?" said Rafe Ashton. "What's this Orpheus that you've been writing for old Rico?"

Writing for old Rico? "I wasn't exactly writing it for Rico." But she had, she was; it was Rico's pale face and the archaic Greek beard and the fire-blue eyes in the burnt-out face that she had seen, an Orpheus head, severed from its body. Or alive, a live head (fastened onto shoulders) was certainly not a late-Roman head, a Roman soldier out of an illustration or out of a room of late Pompeian bronzes in a cold hall. He was pulling her sketch-book out of her hand, he was scratching a verse on the last page, "Lend me your sketch-book, I want to write something." But this was not certainly that Rafe, that one was buried under ashes, hard

lava shut him in, though truly he was there, shut in, cov-
ered over, to be dug out, sometime maybe.

But that was far away, sitting on a red-plush bench
opposite the Venus de Milo in the Louvre. He was sitting
there, but buried under the debris of a roof fallen in, of
books fallen on the floor, of various other sorts of Very
lights, of volcanoes bursting; a tidal wave. He was shuffling
books, papers, on the table.

"Where is it?"

"What?"

"This thing you wrote for Rico?"

"I didn't particularly write it for Rico," she repeated,
seeing the pale face, the burnt eyes, hearing the words that
flamed alive, blue serpents on the page that Rico wrote her,
that were just ordinary letters that you could chuck across a
breakfast-tray to any husband, but that yet held the flame
and the fire, the burning, the believing.

"I don't think I have it," she said—"I think maybe I
sent it in a letter."

"Sent it in a letter?"

"Well, you know, writing a letter—one writes—" and
she knew that the flame and the brand of this gift that Rafe
and Julia had had between them was a secondary refracted
light, the light of a second reflection of the rainbow, not the
blaze and the blue-flame of the sun-shelf. Rico.

"Is this it?"

"I don't know. Those are all discarded pages."

Word shattered and the black earth shattered
over us, your glance, sent hellward. No trance of star-

ing eye-balls can re-invoke the doom, hung over us.
Don't, don't look back.

Go on. Fortunate people in high fields stoop si-
lently, not knowing what they pluck, the heady wine
of not-being on the earth, the heady sensuous tideless
sort of mirth, the flowing over and the holding down, a
being dead, not-dead, sundered and lost still cries don't,
don't look back.

Go on into the upper land of light.

"Not so good," said Rafe Ashton.

"I didn't mean it to be good. It's only the preliminary
scribbling. You remember how I scribbled in a note-book
under that flowering pear at Capri? It's that sort of auto-
matic writing. Out of that if I go on at that, something (on
the back of an envelope) may come."

Swift hunter, hunted by the hand of fate, remorse-
less by the battling of the eight unglorified furies, ever
follows hate. Hate, love not. Let the opening gate lead
you to the upper world, your world of sun and sunlight,
your bright peak of gold bough laced with gold bough,
all the fruit lies waiting for you, waiting for your hand
that plucks the lyre, to pluck; listen not, Orpheus.

Look not again, this last look is the first. Let this
first glance be last-glance for the tithes of winnowing
fate will ask the other-half, the self you know there in
the upper earth has gold of wheat, has wheat and oat
and brass of hanging leaf and old-gold of the harvests,
has no lost dark-red pomegranate seed as once Per-
sephone, vanquished, tasted. Let me taste no blood-red

seed, no, let me say this last, last word to make the
severance complete. Go, Orpheus, look not back.

"A bit dramatic, I don't like your *look not back*. It's
Victorian."

"The whole thing is—I told you, I saved that only for
the other-side of the page, the paper. I kept it for the other-
side of the page, for the paper," she said.

"There aren't eight furies and why unglorified furies?"
he said. There were eight furies, there were eighty furies,
everything was unglorified. She didn't say anything. It
didn't really matter.

"It doesn't really matter."

"What doesn't matter?"

"Why, what I told you, I told you it was only prelim-
inary scribbling."

There was no taut nerve in her that wanted to spring
forward, she had no tragedy-queen desire to stand, facing
him, hand dramatically held forward to seize the maligned
page. She felt no Muse. What does Rafe want, anyway?

"What does Frederick want, what does old Frederico
want with you?" He spoke as if she were a cast-off old
potato-bag or bit of sacking. Did he? No. He spoke as if he
cared, as if it mattered that Rico was writing her, that she
was writing Rico.

"Well, he writes to everybody, his letters are around
somewhere if I kept them, they're there in that stack of
papers." Were they? No. They were burning in her head,
blue-fire, the things he wrote and the things that he didn't

write, the way the blue-flame licked out of the paper, whatever it was he wrote.

"He's cerebral, he has to write to someone."

"Here is no flower—I like this one beginning, here is no flower, better." What did all this matter? "Give it to me." He handed the paper to her. There was her writing, simply the uneven lightning of her lines reached in long, short lines across paper. Sheet lightning. Blue lightning. She had been struck by lightning. Breathed out in this city, turning like a rat in a cage round and round this room with its memories, she had escaped the last manifestation of Rafe-on-leave, the last one. She had not written Rico of Bella but he must have felt something. He must have known that things were different.

"Go back to your frozen altars," he said. Why frozen? She supposed she was frozen—protected, so that the actuality of the fact Rafe-Bella didn't really get through, it was simply some play, some charade, something that happened last leave definitely, that might not happen ("I don't suppose I'll come back") again. "There is no flower—" she read from the loose leaf of blue-lined paper, salvaged from the old note-book.

Here is no flower, however sweet the scent, how deep blood-red, how purple-blue the tint, can bring the life that thyme can, growing drift on drift by a rock, your rock is burnt-sun in that upper light, the grain glows and the inner heart of rock gives heat. Stay on the upper earth and breathe wine from the golden leaf as from a cup, drink deep of herb and sweet-grass, of the grass that grows in long tress in the shorter grass, collect husk of broken acorn-nut, ash twigs, a heap of elderberry skeleton-finger, wood fingers of the last year's blossom; set a light to bramble of the last year's bush, then think, this bramble held a flower shaped like quince, like rose or apple, but the flame lights up to-morrow's blossom, elder, quince and grape. Unknot the woody stem of last year's vine, twist garlands of the dead-wood, do not think that present look or nod or word or breath can reach me in this cavern under-earth. Here it is dark. You are above, in light, touch not your fingers to your harp, your lyre would conjure me, I am not even a ghost with ghost-limbs who might walk, a moment in the moonlight when the moon is crescent, when moonlight is dim, I am not ghost, not even moon-maiden. Touch not your lyre, nor seek to wake what lies forgotten.

"You might boil this one down," he said, "about quarter the length and cut out the *clichés.*"

"Listen," he said, "it's perfectly clear; I love you, I desire *l'autre.*"

Yes, that was clear. The room was clear, it was her room, their room, there had never been any parties, the chrysanthemums were tawny suns, were dark-red and frayed yellow with no flower scent, but the leaf-scent of the woods.

They were trees in various gold and red autumn-leaf, not flowers.

There was a shape to their marriage, broken now, shattered actually, yet there was a shape to it. It was Frederick who had taken her away (cerebrally), it was Bella who had broken across (physically), but all the same, there it was, the union, the two minds that yet had the urge, or the cheek you might say, to dare to communicate. For her, it was very simple.

Rafe the last times back here, had simply not been Rafe but someone else and what does it matter that a strange officer on leave spends half the day upstairs in the little attic bedroom, that Ivan had, that Ivan in Petrograd had bequeathed, so to speak, to Bella Carter whom he had loved at one time, and wanted to be with again? Ivan, Bella? That was clear enough and Rafe, Julia?

But Ivan was in Petrograd and the Rafe that stayed upstairs with Bella was not this Rafe, he did not have this camel-hair dressing-gown that was the colour of the smaller two flowers that were edged with gold like painted paper-flowers at a carnival. The flowers, though they had seemed meaningless, scentless and over-conventional, when she found them this afternoon on the table, were yet symbol, not the most ardent of the flowers they loved together, but symbol, something he had stopped to get, thinking of her, after having been with Bella.

The grim unlovely spectre vanished. Almost it was, as if they were together for the first time, as if Bella had completed him in some purely physical way, as if Rico with his "We will go away together where the angels come down to earth" had completed her, in her purely emotional-cerebral dimension. She had not told Rafe of that letter. Victorian, had he said? Yes, she had locked up that and one or two others in the red-plush lined leather jewel-box that she had got in Florence. Inside the box was the portrait of her mother, with the hair dressed high, 1880 and Victorian. There was the little arrow run through her bodice, the sleeves were tight to the elbow and the bare arms were folded on the conventional back of a chair.

Yes, she was old-fashioned (her mother was old-fashioned) but Rico's flaming letters had been no ordinary love-letters, they were written to her in "pure being," as he said. And Bella had taken away the over-physical sensuality of Rafe so that now, almost for the first time, for the first time anyhow since the ordeal in the nursing-home, she was with him without fear. Almost, Bella Carter had given her back Rafe.

It was not that she thought of Rico; but the fact that Rico wanted her, no matter how idealistically she might translate his letters, meant that there was something there, something that was wanted. Of course Rico did not really want her; he was harassed and distressed and he loved Elsa, his great Prussian wife. He loved Elsa, yes, he said so; no, he did not say so. But it was now as if this cerebral contact had renewed her. She had not actually met Rico (he was in Cornwall) since the writing of the letter, you are a living spirit in a living spirit city. Yes, she was that. Rafe Ashton is my husband.

Wife, husband. Elsa and Rico were very near, she and Rico would burn away, cerebralistically, they would burn out together.

Julia existed, parasitically on Rafe, and Rico lived on Elsa.

But once alive, fed as it were from these firm-fleshed

bodies, they were both free, equal too, in intensity, matched, mated. She did not think of Rico. But it was reading Rico's letter that had started their talk on poetry and she and Rafe had that together.

Bella had nothing of that; Rafe might write poems to Bella, but he and Bella were different. It was poetry that had brought Rafe to her, in the beginning; it was poetry that gave back Rafe now.

He was sleeping. She could feel the even in-drawn breath, the rhythmic out-breathing. She was on the outside of the bed, she could get out. She disentangled herself from the sheets, she stood on her feet. She groped for the matches and the candle that she kept in readiness by her bed, in case of sudden air-alarm or in case that steady pulse and throb that was her head, rather than her heart beating, should command her. *Bid me to live and I will live.* It was something in the distance (Rico was in Cornwall) that empowered her, so that in the middle of the night she could strike a match, and crouched over her bed-clothes, run her pencil down a page, or rather let it run for her. She had sent copies of the poems to Rico, she had not to Rafe. She had stacked a slender sheaf of the typed finished verses in the hollow, back of the books, a *cache*, in the second book-shelf to the right, where the tops of the French books, the yellow-backed *Mercure de France* volumes were low enough to let her hand slide in. It was something secret, something hidden, you might say, even from herself.

She set the lighted candle on the table. Rafe Ashton was still sleeping.

V

The floor-board between the book-case and the rug was cold. She slid her fingers along the top of the *Mercure de France* volumes, pulled one out, pulled out another. She turned to get her slippers, the floor was so cold. Now it seemed like Christmas, the bunch of chrysanthemums was like a little tree. The candle threw its circle of halo-light. Spot-light showed a heap of untidy books, the usual ash-trays; "Kick over your tiresome house of life," Rico had written her. What did he really know about her house of life?

What was the sheaf of poems but an effort at readjustment between true reality and the dreariness of this present? The poems were abstractions really. She would leave the poems for the moment. It was Rafe that mattered, it was that little tree with the great globes of gold and red and russet, like ripe fruit. In her "house of life" that Rico didn't really guess at, was this Tree. Season of mists—certainly—and mellow fruitfulness. She saw that the great yellow globe that caught the candle-flame was perfectly round as her eyes misted. It was an orange on a tree, oranges and apples, or just Christmas-tree balls with a candle.

Something was born between them, between Rafe and herself, the Christ-child of their battered integrity, of something they had, of the straightforward way they had of telling each other everything.

Yes, she preferred to have known, straight, about what he and Bella were up to, in that little room upstairs. What did any of that matter? What did Rico matter with his blood-stream, his sex-fixations, his man-is-man, woman-is-woman? That was not true. This mood, this realm of consciousness was sexless, or all sex, it was child-consciousness, it was heaven. In heaven, there is neither marriage nor giving in marriage. They were, they had been, she and Rafe, homeless; they had found each other. This man-, this woman-theory of Rico's was false, it creaked in the joints. Rico could write elaborately on the woman mood, describe women to their marrow in his writing; but if she turned round, wrote the Orpheus part of her Orpheus-Eurydice sequence, he snapped back, "Stick to the woman-consciousness, it is the intuitive woman-mood that matters." He was right about that, of course. But if he could enter, so diabolically, into the feelings of women, why should not she enter into the feelings of men? She understood Rafe, really understood that he loved her—that he desired *l'autre*.

L'autre was out on the wild or *l'autre* was alone upstairs, maybe even now waiting for Rafe to join her. Oh, it was all a muddle. But no, it was not. There was the candle and its exact circle of light, an exact geometrical definition, as exact as the clock-dial on the clock, as the little circle on the watch he had strapped round her wrist, the time before the time before the last (was it?), late winter or early spring anyhow, and this was autumn and the war would sometime be over.

The war will never be over. Walk straight out, put the two books now on the table, for Rafe is sitting up in bed, he will ask what she is doing.

"I went over to the shelves to get some books," she said, though she need not have said anything; the two yellow-backed paper volumes were clasped against her nightdress, a child with a Christmas package, at dawn.

"What is this about you and old Rico?"

"Oh—nothing—I mean—I told you—" but she had not told him. She put the yellow-backed books on the table; the gold of the globe-flower, the cone-shape of the yellow candle-flame, the halo of light, were separate golds, different yellow-gold. The candle-flame was paler. The edge of the outer ring just touched the edge of the bed. It was a painting, they were a picture, drawn here, outlined here, something hung on the wall in the *Scuolo di San Rocco* in Venice. It was misted over, dim, a picture that had been hanging a long time. There was none of this stark Attic frozen marble, none of the late-Roman destructive bronze. It was natural, normal, it was stage-set but it was real.

She seemed to have been acting a part with her "You must do as you think best," with her "That is Bella's affair," with her "Try to be more careful, it isn't as if I minded but it would be rather dreadful if Miss Ames asked us to leave." Her latest concern had not been "Are they together, aren't they?" but "I hope now they are together, they'll have the sense not to make too much noise on the stairs as they did last time when they came in." That was a terrible time, the worst, but after that nothing had mattered, she took it all for granted.

Really, it had not been his staying up there, spending his precious afternoons away, it was that last time when they came in so late and she left the door open a crack and he had not come in. His not coming in that time, just to say good-night, had been a worse blow than any of all the rest, as if he had not trusted her, not trusted himself, or as if Bella simply dragged him along up the stairs, which was worse than if he himself had done it. It was the last link with him; the disintegration, she had told herself, was complete.

But this afternoon she had found the flowers on the table and now in this short time all the rest had vanished, the flowers had blossomed mysteriously, or given out heady scent of woods and wild spaces, of snow falling softly on peaked roofs, of a picture from a picture-book, the *Little Match Girl* with the last match. That last candle that had been that last straw, that last match. But that was long ago, last night, night before last, and things, as they had a way of doing these days, went on in various dimensions, so that this was perfect, and there had never been a Bella nor Morgan le Fay nor any of those parties.

"Why don't you tell me—Julia?"

Why don't I tell him? Tell him what? She came alive; in the soft penumbra of the candle, she fed on the soft maize-gold of the candle-circle. She was alive. She sat down on the edge of the bed.

"You never gave all of yourself to me, there was Lett Barnes first."

"There was Morgan," was the answer to that but she did not want to spoil the mellow painting hung on the wall outside the chapel of the *Scuolo di San Rocco* in Venice. There was (is) Morgan. But that did not matter. She did not want to spoil the maize-gold mood that was a candle on a table, a tall single candle that made up for that stub of a candle-end she had left burning (last night?) with the door open a crack, so that he would come in, just to say good-night, on his way upstairs with Bella.

"Lett Barnes was long ago; and anyhow," she managed, "I was never really with Lett."

"Were you ever really with anybody?"

"To-night," she said, "with you."

"Were you? Aren't you always going off—thinking—I never know what you are thinking."

"Does anyone ever know what anyone is thinking?"

"Well—with Bella I know—"

Did he? How could he say that? How, at this moment of ultimate perfection, could he drag in Bella? It was Rico, really, that he was thinking of, he was worried about Rico. Well, tell him about Rico.

"It started—I don't know how it started. I mean—it didn't. He was the only one who seemed remotely to understand what I felt when I was so ill—well—it was long ago, I know. But he understood that."

"We all understood that."

Let him have it his own way. They didn't. No one had understood but Rico.

"He came several times to the flat in Hampstead when you were out. He watched me once peeling apples in one of those Spanish pottery bowls—they're all down in the basement now. I should get out more of the dishes," she said.

"What else?"

"Nothing else. He said he liked my Greek renderings better than Gilbert Murray; he said that there was a bite and sting in my writing—but he must have said that when we were all together. He sent me a cardboard box with some little lettuce-plants he had grown in his garden in Cornwall and some sea-pinks last summer. In a carboard box," she repeated.

"You didn't tell me about the sea-pinks and the lettuces," he said.

"Didn't I? Well, he did. He sent me a manuscript of one of his novels, but it seemed very long, very confused, I must have written you about it. Then when I was alone— when was it?—maybe last spring after you left—no, it was at Corfe Castle, he wrote, *we must go away where the angels come down to earth.*" Here, the angels came down to earth.

"Go away?"

"Well—not go away—you know what he's like. He talks of going away. I suppose he wrote a dozen people. Maybe he didn't. Maybe he wrote just me. Anyhow that is what he wrote."

"What did you write him?"

"I don't know. I sent him some poems. That's how we began really to write. You said I should go on writing. He said I should go on writing—"

"Well, yes," said Rafe Ashton, "you should go on writing."

Now he pushed out of the bed. He drew the camel-hair dressing-gown around him, now he was knotting the cord, this was Rafe, this was Anthony, this was the thing under

the Christmas-tree (where the angels come down to earth),
this was bid me to live and I will live, this was—this was—

He seemed to have snapped into something. He seemed
to be older in a minute. She looked up and saw for the first
time a grown man, someone older, at last or for the mo-
ment, more authoritative, someone who was at last making
some gesture to all this, who was not simply saying "I won't
come back, I can't discuss this now, you must leave me alone
at least this time, you know how terrible it is, I'm going
back to-morrow." For the first time, in a long time, he
seemed to be facing up to something.

"If I don't come back—" he was saying in a different
way—"or if I do come back—do you love Frederick?"

Do I love Rico? Do I love Frederico? Do I love old
Rico?

"No, not at this minute. He is part of the cerebral burn-
ing, part of the inspiration. He takes but he gives."

"Didn't I give?"

"Yes—everything— No, not everything. Nobody gives
anybody everything. There was Morgan."

"I thought you liked Fay, she's very fond of you."

"Yes, so Rico said, too. Rico said to me, 'You seem to
mean a great deal to Morgan le Fay.' Well—Morgan—"
This was the last person she wanted to talk about.

She could not tell Rafe that it was the casual taking-for-
granted of Morgan coming in and spending the night, of
her way of throwing her arms about Rafe that had started
the whole thing. She had thought when Bella came along,
well, at least Bella is straight in her way; in her crooked
definition, she is straight, while Morgan lolls about and you

never know what it is she wants; she makes half-love to me. Bella is at least straight. She leaves me out of it. Her "it's all or nothing" was at least direct, you knew where you were. At least you knew when he was upstairs with Bella— while Morgan— But don't think of Morgan.

It was the suave insinuations of Morgan that made Julia at last feel that anything was better than drifting along in the web of sophisticated love-making, "I think it would be so lovely to have a woman-lover," when how could Morgan say that? If she wanted women, let her have women, not use women, as Julia felt she did, as a sort of added touch of exoticism, something to stir and excite, not really knowing what she meant, only wanting to web over everything with the maze and tangle of her long fair hair, her enticing crêpe de chine, the mille-fleurs that she had recognized on Rafe's sleeves, before Bella came into it. But that couldn't have surprised her. She had seen it often enough, Morgan with her arms around him, and her "Oh, darling, it's really women I love."

"What's Morgan got to do with all this?"

"Nothing—" But she remembered it was Morgan who had first said, "But Rico loves you."

It was all right in the beginning. But as the war crept closer, as it absorbed everything, the thing that bound body and soul together seemed threatened, so that she seemed to tune-in to another dimension, a world where she walked alone with an image and that image was Rico. Truly, yes, she loved him but loved him in another dimension, out of the body, wandering in thought, in dream, Rico himself had written "You are entangled in your own dream."

But this was reality.

"Do I love him? Yes—no. Why? Of course, you know I am waiting, have been waiting for you. You changed, of course. I can't go into that now."

He was talking to her. Now, himself, Rafe Ashton, was also of that dream. Now dream and reality merged; he was saying all the things that he had said before. He was speaking their own language, but with a definite objective, not as if he were talking to fill in time.

"Cigarette?" He was looking for the matches. All that —those first cigarettes that she had smoked for the first time, with him, in Italy.

"I don't know. I don't think so."

"Yes," he said, and "I'm making tea. We can't sit here shivering. I'm going away to-morrow."

To-morrow and to-morrow and to-morrow. It was the same scene, the same picture, it was herself and Rafe Ashton, for the last time.

For the last time or the first? Well, Bella at least had been some definite sort of acid, something stark and acrid, straightforward. She took love-making utterly for granted. No nuances. "Funny, in the old days"—it was already the old days—Bella had said, "people asked us to a dance or to have a dance; now they simply say, will you sleep with me." Did they? That was the world Bella had fallen into in Paris, the world she had whirled about in, sky-rocket, green flame.

But Bella was an art-student from America, just starting, getting a foot-hold, living with her mother in a studio near the river, gay enough, but certainly from Ivan's account, nothing like this Bella. Or this Bella was simply the original one, projected out, projected into its most dynamic manifestation, hot-house growth, forced to live many lives, many loves to the even-worse sound (in Paris) of shrapnel.

Julia was like Bella in that, in the opposite dimension, also projected out, but projected into an even more dangerous world of dreams ("entangled in your own dream," as Rico put it), simply projected off from the other end of the see-saw, or likely to be bounced off at any minute, with Rafe Ashton in the centre, up you go, Bella, down you go Julia, holding hands, changing partners.

But this was not a party, not even the aftermath of a party. She hadn't troubled to see people, this time. Bella and Rafe made it outrageously obvious that they only wanted to sneak off and be together, leaving her with the lovely wifely part of camouflaging love-affair for husband-on-leave. No. This was the last time.

For the situation, he said, was impossible. I love you, I desire *l'autre*, was impossible. Or was it, according to Rafe Ashton, very simple? "I want to be with Bella;" well, be with Bella. But Bella? You can not play this game of geometrical abstractions with a person of Bella's temperament. At first she had said, "This always happens to me, men don't really like me, they always get tired of me." Now she was saying, "It's all or nothing; you tyrannize Rafe's spirit." That is what she said. Bella had something to say now, and she was not behindhand, not reticent in saying it, "It's all or nothing." And Rafe was saying, "I'll go mad, I am torn to pieces, I love you." Was it all play-acting? Or did he really mean it? Well, to-night, at any rate, he meant it.

And to-night was to-night, and even to-night was not entirely secure. Unconsciously, she was alert; she was waiting for the sound of the warning, of the air-raid warning. Her outer mind, frozen on the top, would go on quietly, this day and this day. But underneath, she was shot to bits—they all were—waiting for the end. The war will never be over.

Thinner, taller, he looked standing now by the table. Yes, they might as well sit up now for the rest of the night, have something out between them. "I will go mad." He looked sane enough, he was certainly detached enough. "I want Bella. Bella makes me forget. You make me remember." Well, there was at least that to her credit, she had kept the flame alight, this candle on the table. She had kept something alive between them, the ilex-trees of the Pincio, the thin Byzantium columns of the outer courtyard of Saint John Lateran—if it was St. John—at Rome. The very substance of the ancient marble torso in that garden.

"Do you remember that garden?" she said, now playing her old game of keeping the torch lighted.

"What garden, Julie?" He spoke to her tenderly as if she were a child, a child in a fairy-tale, talking of a garden.

"Oh, that garden outside the—whatever it was—museum; you know, where they had the plaque, that beautiful frozen fury."

"Oh, Michelangelo," he said; and she knew they were at their old game, he had not forgotten, he did not want to forget.

"Yes, I was thinking of Michelangelo, not that the fury was—" but he knew that perfectly. "I was thinking that our hands had run over that marble torso as they said Michelangelo's did after he had gone blind."

Yes—that was it, the very touch of the fingers of Michelangelo had been transferred to theirs. Their feet, their hands were instilled with living beauty, with things that were not dead. Other cities had been buried. Other people had been shot to death and something had gone on. There was something left between them.

"The trouble with you, Julie, was, you always lived a world ahead."

What a thing to say.

"It sounds like something out of Dante." Was it Dante? Certainly, there were concentric, geometric exactly-patterned circles of hell for them, for all of them. For Bella, for Morgan, for Rico, for Elsa a pre-war Prussian whose famous junker brother had lately crashed as they all were bound to crash, sooner or later. A world ahead? What did he mean by that? Or was it a world behind? Or did the past, the past circles of worlds, the steps of the temple of Poseidon at Poseidonia, the flower-stalk columns of that arcade of marble columns of Saint John Lateran at Rome (or wherever it was) remain even after they were bombed to hell, one way or another, a pattern in the air? Were there worlds that remained, worlds of past beauty that were future beauty? Did the past and the future blend (or would they) in one eternal circle of the absolute, of final beauty? That prayer they quoted (from Plato, was it?), *And may the inner and the outer be at peace.* Here, certainly there was no peace, or peace so hardly won in these rarer moments of fulfilment that they became worlds ahead; as he said, as Rico said, "You are entangled in your own dream." Was, or wasn't it the dream that mattered?

He was looking for the tea-box. "It's over there by the books." He found it. It was the same tea-box with the cracked enamel figures, a Chinaman and the usual geisha with a parasol.

"We ought somehow to have collected somewhere, or someone should have given us a really elegant red-lacquer box with two compartments inside, of tin or zinc or whatever it is, and one of those little bone spoons."

He said, "Yes, there are a lot of things people should have given us."

"Well, they gave us a good deal, there's that imitation jade Buddha that Mrs Mount-Seaton gave us, the one that Savage Landor gave her great-aunt."

"Yes."

They laughed. It was an old joke.

"People always thought (in the beginning) that we so frightfully belonged," he said.

But why look back? There was only this evening, this night, this morning, there was only now. And already the kettle was simmering on the gas-ring, already he was saying, "You'll catch cold, Julie," already he was finding, had found, his army great-coat, which he dropped over her shoulders.

"That's the stuff to give the troops," said Rafe Ashton.

VI

There he sat, the little man. He was hunched up in her arm-chair. She was facing him in the other arm-chair. Elsa had gone off with Bella. They liked Bella. She had taken Elsa off to do some shopping. Elsa had said, "I'll leave Frederico with you." It was understood, Elsa had given them, as it were, her blessing; she and Rico were to work something out between them. But Rico was so dreadfully tired. She was not even tired, she had got past being tired. She didn't feel anything. Rafe Ashton was right, "You don't feel anything."

The little man was not so little really. He stood almost as tall as she when they stood face to face. He was not going to give in. They had taken his cottage, they had taken his manuscripts, they had warned him that he could not come back to Cornwall.

"It's you, your fault, you damn Prussian," he had shouted at Elsa, yesterday, over dinner. They had spread an impromptu meal on the table there and Bella had come in, and really there wasn't any problem. Not any problem of Orpheus, shattered; that was poetry. The problem simply was, where should the Fredericks stay, who would house them? Of course, they could manage here for a few days, Rico upstairs in Ivan's room, Bella and Elsa there on the couch, herself on the little camp-bed back of the screen. What more could anyone ask?

Someone, sooner or later, would turn up with a place for the Fredericks; already he said, "I'm sorry, Molly Croft wasn't at home this morning when I went to Hampstead; but she still has the cottage in Kent, she wrote that we could go there. Her son, on leave, is there."

"But he'll be going back," said Julia.

It was the old pattern, someone on leave, someone going back, someone who might not come back. Now they had to think of Molly Croft and her son.

For the moment this would do. Rafe wouldn't be back again for some time, if he ever came back again. There was no problem. There was the problem of "scrounging," as Rafe would have put it, enough to eat, there was the problem of Miss Ames who had suddenly turned on her in the hall last night, "But Mrs Ashton, you never told me that Mrs Frederick is a German."

There he sat. He had poured himself, at volcanic heat, into his novels, those heady sex-expositions that nobody would publish, after his last novel had been suppressed. That had happened just at the beginning of the war. But anyhow, people weren't publishing that sort of novel now. His poems were written at the same state of molten-lava temperature, but now the lava was cool, ashes fell almost visibly upon them. He was tired out. She was. They were cold, not with indifference but with a sort of understanding. I am not this person, I am the person who sent you the sea-pinks in the box; there was all of me in the manuscript which you didn't even trouble to write me about, more than the mere acknowledgment of its arrival.

Here I am, the other one seemed to say, you don't know what has been going on in this room for the last six months, off and on, but you do know everything. Here I am, but really I am tied up in the rough copy of the poems hidden behind the *Mercure de France* volumes. I sent you most of them. But that is me. This isn't.

They did not say any of this. The mud was still stuck to his rough ploughman boots, his corduroy trousers were tucked in at the tops. He had not even had time to shake, as it were, the dust off his feet. Cornwall was still with him. The sea-tan, sun-tan, had not withered from his face; but for all that, one felt the pallor beneath it. Soon he would be white and drawn, as he had been the first time she saw him, visibly an invalid, with his narrow chest, his too-flaming beard, his blue eyes. The eyes looked at her, not surprised to see her, as if he had been there a long time.

They didn't seem to have anything to say to one another. Last night, he had sat there and Elsa had sat in the chair where Julia was now sitting and Julia had sat like a good child between them. "Elsa is there," said Rico, "you are here. Elsa is there at my right hand," he said. "You are here," he said, while Elsa went on placidly hemming the torn edge of an old jumper. Her work-bag spilled homely contents on

the floor. Their bags, the few belongings they had had time
to get together, all they now had, were stacked against the
book-shelf, the other side of the room.

There were the usual tea-cups. Rico didn't smoke. Elsa
chain-smoked till all the cigarettes had given out. Rico said,
"You are there for all eternity, our love is written in blood,"
he said, "for all eternity." But whose love? His and Elsa's?
No—that was taken for granted. It was to be a perfect tri-
angle, Elsa acquiesced.

"This will leave me free," she muttered in her German
guttural, "for Vanio."

Who is Vanio? She did not like to ask them. Vanio, it
transpired later, was a certain young Scot, or half-Scot
named Vane, who had the big house not so far from their
house in Cornwall. It appeared he had what they called a
slight tic, not real heart-trouble, but enough to keep him out
of the army.

He was a young composer.

Already, there was this neat pairing off, Rafe, Bella—
though she herself had told them nothing—Rico, Julia, and
to show that it was all neat and rounded off, or perfectly
squared and tidy at the edges, there was this vague distant
young musician who was coming up to town to be with
them, at Christmas. Well, Christmas was not so far off. But
somehow the blood and eternity touch, though really Rico
seemed to mean it, seemed too much; as if neither Julia nor
Rico could really live up to it, to anything of that sort,
though obviously he and Elsa had it all fixed up between
them.

Julia looked at Rico and his eyes were not far-off, they
were not vague, they were a real-blue (in his tanned face)

with a glint of lapis. They were not cold eyes, they were not calculating. Perhaps if Julia had been other, she would have sensed the whole of last night's scene as unreal, not artificial but somehow out of the world, naïf in its expressed intention. Elsa had or would have or had had a young friend (lover?), a musician; this fitted in with Rico's great goddess-mother idea of her and did not break across their own relationship. Elsa had fed Rico on her "power," it was through her, in her, and around her that he had done his writing. Well, here was this Vanio, another artist, younger, another member of this odd troupe.

Julia saw that Rico was looking at his knapsack, the other side of the room. "What do you want?" But he did not answer. He simply got up and unearthed a note-book and felt in his pockets that looked as if they should hold a screw of raffia for tying up a bush, a small pruning-knife. He found his pencil.

Well, he was writing. That seemed to be all that mattered. He had spread the note-book open on his knee and was scribbling away, simply all-there, like a little schoolmaster setting an examination or correcting an exercise, she thought, the true artist working with no apparent self-consciousness. He must feel at home here, she thought, and moved away to the far side of the room, lest in some way her presence there might cut across, or he might look up, thinking he had par politesse to make some remark; not that that was likely. She did not trouble to look out a book, sat, her face toward the window, where the plane-trees were swaying in the wind, their branches etched against the near sky.

"The sky is too near," Rico had oddly said one of those times they had talked together in Hampstead, walking back from the borrowed cottage in the Vale of Health to their flat. "The sky is too near. I hate the sky in England, it's paper," he said, "damp blotting-paper."

She remembered that now, as she watched the plane-trees with their decoratively peeled bark and their stark skeleton branches. There was never enough snow in England. She found herself thinking of snow and remembering the broken fragment of a Dodona poem she had written; it was there in the little roll of poems at her elbow, behind those books. It was still there.

Un-numbered seasons and the flakes that glide in single purpose, she remembered. Those upright columns of her constant preoccupation. That was funny about Rico, he shouted at her, "Kick over your tiresome house of life," he wrote, "our languid lily of virtue nods perilously near the pit;" yet when it came to one, any one, of her broken stark metres, he had no criticism to make. She would get out the poems. She would go over the poems. Her eyes followed the line of a plane-tree branch, etched on a flat screen.

Then she looked up to find a trail, a communication between them. It was marked in the dim grey afternoon light of this same room, simply a track across the room, his eyes meeting her eyes. How long had he been watching her? From the moment she turned to the window, to let her thought veer off, run along the line of that plane-tree branch? Her thought, projected outward, had yet been circumscribed by the uneven algebraic formula of that branch.

She imagined that he had turned to look at her, the moment she was so thoroughly detached that her thought went back to the Dodona poem; she might have been alone then. Yet thinking of the Dodona poem, she had been nearer to the Rico that had projected it in her, or out of her; the Rico absent was nearer than the Rico present.

And now, here was this track between them, written in the air, not fiery, but imbued with some familiar magnetism. Not tense and taut, not tense as she had felt him to be, throwing out his strange and somehow theatrical statement last night, his "written in blood for all eternity." Not written in blood, written in this grey city air, in this dim room, where so much else had happened, yet written for all eternity.

She got up; as if at a certain signal, she moved toward him; she edged the small chair toward his chair. She sat at his elbow, a child waiting for instruction. Now was the moment to answer his amazing proposal of last night, his "for all eternity." She put out her hand. Her hand touched his sleeve. He shivered, he seemed to move back, move away, like a hurt animal, there was something untamed, even the slight touch of her hand on his sleeve seemed to have annoyed him. Yet, last night, sitting there, with Elsa sitting opposite, he had blazed at her; those words had cut blood and lava-trail on this air. Last night, with the coffee-cups beside them on the little table, he had said "It is written in blood and fire for all eternity." Yet only a touch on his arm made him shiver away, hurt, like a hurt jaguar.

He was leopard, jaguar. It was not she who had started out to lure him. It was himself with his letters, and last night his open request for this relationship. Yet even this touch (not heavy on his sleeve) seemed to send some sort of repulsion through him. She drew back her hand. There were voices at the door.

She did not know, would she ever know, whether his gesture had been personal repugnance, some sort of *noli me tangere* (his own expression) or whether his over-subtle awareness had sensed this interruption. Elsa and Bella were laughing, they had met Miss Ames on the stairs, "the little dragon," as Elsa called her, who had been so acid on the subject of Elsa, a German just last night, was already inquiring about Frederick. "What did you do to her?" said Elsa. "But he has those ways," said Elsa, sensing or not sensing this thing in the room, the poignant moment not so much shattered or broken, but simply shelved, put aside, put away somewhere, smudged out, as if a cloth had run over a diagram on a black-board.

Julia did not move away, she sat just where she had been sitting, hands folded on her lap, that hand that his arm (under the rough tweed) had shivered away from, just five, ten seconds ago, that hand lay on her lap, and she did not stiffen, she did not feel herself draw erect, nor turn in any self-conscious effort toward readjustment. The room was full of Elsa, her thick, rich voice flowed over them. Julia's back was turned, but she felt Bella moving things on the table. It would be tea-time again.

Elsa was saying, "Buns, bear-buns for the lion." And Rico had his pencil; had he held it all this time, or had he laid it down between the open covers of his old-fashioned school exercise-book, when he turned to face her? He was writing as if nothing at all had happened; not looking up, the pencil went on.

"Buns," shouted Elsa, as if they were all deaf, over-working her hearty Teutonic witticism "for the li-ioon, I tell you," and she moved round to face them. "Frederico, I ask you, that little dragon, she said, 'and ho-oow' is . . . ,'" imitating with her guttural German the somewhat distinguished English of the little Fabian. It didn't sound the least bit like Miss Ames speaking. "She said," Elsa repeated, "how is your famous husband," but Miss Ames would never have said anything so obvious, implied it perhaps, making some kind of gesture toward Elsa for her un-Fabian outburst of county British sentiment last night. "What, I ask you, Frederico, did you do—put down that damn pencil." Would or would he not put down the pencil? He did not.

Elsa fumbled along the mantel-edge for matches. "I got some of my very own old-time fags," she said, "like old times, pre-this-damn-war, Bella found me in the shop." Elsa found matches, she fumbled in her hand-bag for the packet of cigarettes, she lighted a cigarette like a booted Uhlan. She puffed smoke through her nostrils.

"Ah-hhh—" she sighed deeply. "What have you and Frederico been doing?" she asked Julia.

"Oh, nothing, he was writing."

"Ah-hh—" puffed Elsa, with the justifiable pride of a barn-yard hen who has hatched a Phoenix, "we never pay any attention to that writing." But her very words were singularly protective and Rico went on writing.

He looked up. "Miss Ames?" he said.

"Yes—Frederico," I said, "what did you do with your female-twisting magic" (was that one under the belt for Julia) "that you make her to smile actually and say, 'Aha, and how, Mrs Frederick, is your famous husband this evening?' "— and so on and so on. Elsa went on with her charade, elaborating now a gesture of the cigarette that distantly recalled Miss Ames and her amber holder.

Rico said, "I told her she'd changed her beads."

"Beads?" said Bella from the table.

"Yes," said Rico. "Last night she had on Venetian glass-beads, she had on some other glass-beads this afternoon. I said (on the stairs) 'Miss Ames, what a beautiful collection you must have, I think I like these even better than the ones you wore last night.' " He flung his head back with a malicious little giggle, "That fetched her."

So he was "fetching" people, was he? No fish was too small for his net, was it? Julia was suddenly repelled by the mask he seemed suddenly to clap on his face; it was a carved mask, she had seen it somewhere. It was the Rubens' red of his beard, or Titian. The mouth (now that he laughed like that) made him Satyr. There, suddenly in a second, he was stamped on her mind, the flame of the red beard, aggressive, horn-symbol, horn of plenty. The mouth showed the teeth, not remarkable in any way for symmetry or lack of symmetry, but teeth to tear, to devour. The eyes were wrinkled with his laughter, the eyes were drawn slant-wise up toward the ears. He was volcanic; sun-baked pottery would make a mask of this, painted of course. Round it some Della-Robbia work of woven fruit-branch. *Season of mists and mellow fruitfulness.* This was.

She was astonished by the clarity of her perception.

She pushed back the little chair, it slid easily across the blue carpet to another angle. She could see, without turning her head, Bella shoving things about on the big, untidy table, taking a sort of proprietary air to this room. Well, why not? The room was no longer her home, her own; strange cross-currents had been at work upon it. Elsa's work-bag was lying on the floor by one of the table-legs, there was the untidy heap of half-unpacked bags assembled in a hurry; all that they now had.

"The water, I'm afraid, has given out," she said, making no effort to get up. Bella, as if at home, in this her own room, went behind the screen; she came out with the wash-stand jug. "If you don't mind, Bella." Elsa had flung her coat down on a chair. Someone must assemble tea-cups. A paper-bag lay on the table, those bear-buns for the lion. Elsa went on puffing. Rico was or was not writing. Bella came back. Julia, by an effort, stood, looked round for the kettle. But Bella already had it. "Oh, thank you, Bella."

She sat down again, her eyes saw the Spanish screen but did not see through the Spanish-leather screen; what went on there behind it, was now none of her affair. Bella had taken over, it was really kind of Bella. Why make an effort, any more? Either this was or was not her room, evidently it's a public highway. She was sitting alone in the midst of this confusion.

In a moment, she must make an effort, but for this moment she saw as if drawn on the Spanish screen or rather too-vividly painted, the face of Rico. Rico was sitting by her. She did not turn to look at Rico, for the actual face of Rico was projected out, it was a mask set among fruit-trees. It was

Satyr in a garden. *We will go away where the angels come down to earth.* What sort of angels?

The confusion of the past years, the tension, the under-nourishment, the constant terror, Rafe and his death-fixation, now seemed to vanish. Why care? What, anyhow, did it matter? What, anyhow, did any of them matter? If any one of them mattered, it was obviously Rico in his corduroy trousers, in his thick shoes with the dust literally of Cornwall still upon them, with his flaming beard and his neurotic high-pitched giggle, with his "That fetched her." Julia was projected out; or, rather, sitting there, seemed to focus, see this whole problem, flung like so many magic-lantern pictures on the screen before her.

Of course, it was very simple. Rico was the last drop of acid in this mixture. Here was this seething test-tube; and Rico, simply by his presence in this room, projected out Julia so that there she was. There she could sit, there she could even take command of a situation that was beyond any definition. There she could watch Bella; she stooped to pick up Elsa's work-bag. There was Bella, capable, American, with French veneer; and there was Elsa, a pre-war Prussian of the junker classes, and there was Rico, with incipient T.B., his little house of life come bang down, swept away in the war-tornado; "You damn Prussian, it was all your fault," he had shouted last night at Elsa. But even if it was Elsa's fault, it was wonderful to have Elsa here in this room.

There was Elsa, puffing away like an Uhlan and there was Bella setting out the cups and there was Rico. And just opposite her, if she could find a second in eternity, that was out of time, out of this time, was a series of brightly coloured magic-lantern slides, Rico and herself in another dimension, but a dimension so starkly separate from this room, this city, this war, that it actually seemed to be taking place somewhere else, so that there was no confusion. Deliberately she faced the table, faced Bella, Elsa, turned her back on Rico. Rico was there, his poignant personality had projected out Julia. And Julia was "just there," to use his own expression, when he had made his somewhat over-stressed statement or set forward his proposition, his proposal last night. "Just there, for all eternity."

Eternity was not this come-and-go; the war will never be over. Elsa with her "this damn war," or her cigarettes that were "pre-this-damn-war," was facing matters, competent and Teutonic. Rafe was all over the place, he got down deep, under-sea. But he mixed dimensions. But Rico was safe with his supreme, hard-won, valiant indifference.

Elsa was at-one in her straightforward manner, she was an enemy in a foreign country, she had touched bed-rock. It didn't really matter. She had the flair and the indifference and the independence of her class; her pre-war German distinction seemed to send out waves of warmth, it was Rubens in a gallery. It was she really who had made a sort of aura round Rico, no one of his own people had been able to give him this confidence, it was the old-German attitude, that they jeered at in the daily papers, "kultur" really, if you come to think of it.

Even she, Julia was a woman with some sort of gift, to Elsa; not the supreme gift of her supreme and suprisingly hatched Phoenix, but maybe, it seemed to Julia watching Elsa relight another cigarette from the diminished stub of this last, is was a sort of recognition. It was really, Julia had the sense to realise (her own New England pragmatism) that she was to be used, a little heap of fire-wood, brush-wood, to feed the flame of Rico.

If Julia can feed Rico, Elsa seemed to calculate, with profound and exact Teutonic thoroughness, then why not? It will leave me free for Vanio. It was German. It was not Yankee, it was this new-America perhaps that Bella had found in Paris. Yet there they were, separate elements in a test-tube.

The experiment was under way.

But it was in another, not yet defined dimension. It was herself with inherited New England thoroughness who was perhaps the most experimental, herself part of it, but herself watching the mixture now poured into the test-tube, about to bubble.

It had all happened too suddenly. Life was lived to the very extreme edge of possibility, it was lived dangerously with danger taken-for-granted. But pass the danger point, step over the last-straw edge of everything, and nothing matters, you watch your own body being vivisected and take part, encourage the dissector.

Past the danger point, past the point of any logic and of any meaning, and everything has a meaning. A meaning in another dimension, not even that. Casual meaning in everything, in Elsa's work-bag spilling its homely contents on the floor, Rico looking for a pen-knife, Bella twisting a ribbon for a hat on the chintz-covered settee, on the far side of the room where Julia had sat watching the line of a plane-tree a half-hour ago (was it?) when looking up, she had seen Rico's eyes upon her.

They seemed to be superimposed on one another like a stack of photographic negatives. Hold them up to the light and you get in reverse light-and-shade, Julia and Bella seated on that same chintz-covered couch, a composite, you get Rico seated in Rafe's arm-chair, you get Elsa, Germania, in its largest proportion, superimposed simply on Rule Britannia.

Start superimposing, you get odd composites, nation on nation. It's a dangerous game, unless you are tethered to your own dynamic centre as Rico was tethered (so far, no further) to the totem-pole of Rule Germania. Rico was able to dart out, make his frantic little excursions into any unknown dimension, because there, firm as a rock, was Elsa. He cropped round and round, eating up field-flowers, grass; goat-like, his teeth made furrows in symbolic olive trees. When he had got his full, his genius would demand fresh fields and up would pull the totem-pole, Germania, obligingly plant itself in another meadow. Certainly, no. Julia moved like a ghost about this room, avoiding like missiles in the air the shouted trumpet-notes Rico and Elsa were hurling at one another. "You damn fool Frederico—I can tell you—" and his "shut-up, shut-up, shut-up, you damn Prussian, I don't want to hear anything you can tell me."

Bella tactful and quiet, looked like a wax-work. To-day she was wearing the wide ruffle that made her, with her white make-up, look like a girl-clown in a ballet.

Elsa and Frederick had gone out to join some friends, so Julia had the room to herself at last. She had a lot to do, there was the letter to Rafe. She had not written Rafe the last few days. Even now, she was writing Rafe almost daily. There was a nudge rather than a knock at the door and as she waited, hoping that Miss Ames was not coming in for one of her trying little bouts of gossip, the door opened. Bella stood there in her green frock with the buttons down the front, looking as if she were making a stage entrance. Surely this room was open on one side; everything that went on here, it seemed to Julia, was public property, no privacy, yet with a sort of inner sanctity that public works of art have. They seemed to be acting in a play, yet un-selfconsciously, trained actors who had their exits, their entrances. Well, Julia had nothing to do with anything any more. These exits, these entrances were taken out of her hands.

"Well, Bella?"

She did not mean her voice to sound sharp but her nerves were already frayed past all endurance. This was the first hour for days she had had to herself. "I was just going to write some letters."

Bella turned, the door closed after her.

"Bella."

Bella came back. This was another scene, another set of properties. The same properties.

A curtain had dropped on Elsa, Frederico, Bella, Julia and Miss Ames last night. Rico was rather hectic, Julia thought, being self-consciously the great little man, talking Italian, imitating an Italian waiter for fun, as they got ready the coffee cups for Miss Ames, imitating Miss Ames when she left and doing it very well.

Did he imitate all of them, Julia had wondered while

she watched him doing his little charade (he had done it
before) of himself meeting Miss Ames on the stairs. His
hand went up to his throat with a Medici Venus gesture.
Elsa egged him on.

"But you said la-ast time, Frederico, that she said they
were Venetian."

"Well," he went on, "yes, they were Venetian, I no-
ticed the poor old beads were going threadbare, you know
Venetian beads when they get moth-eaten."

"Oh, yes—and—"

"I told her they were, I knew, from the Piazzetta, not
the main square, and she went on about Florian, of course,
she would. Florian!" Rico, it seemed, put the words into
the mouth of his Scrooge; were they all dummies for Rico?
Rico had the centre of the stage, he was strutting admirably.
There were spots of colour in his face. His voice cracked up
into falsetto,

"Oh, Mr Frederick, how did you *know*—" and he burst
into spinsterish giggles—"that I got them in the Piazzetta?"

Now Bella had entered. Would everyone else do a little
turn, while she watched them, wondering when it would
ever be over? (The war would never be over.)

But Bella came forward; in spite of the wild-rose colour
she had put on to-day to go with that green frock, she was
oddly awkward, like a school-girl dressed up. She was tall,
almost as tall as Julia, her feet were small, she moved with
an awkward self-conscious gesture, like an animal tied up
in clothes, pretty clothes, a deer, gazelle, with her tilted
eyes, that looked out now as if she were suddenly (with all
her veneer of self-conscious sophistication) frightened.

"Come in." Must she shout it through the overtones of
this room that seemed darting with so many colours, as if a

basket of fireworks had gone off leaving a trail of green, red, orange, the dripping shriek-sparks of Rico's unkind yet wholly admirable little piece of imitation? Julia thought of Rico and of his hand suddenly clutching imaginary beads.

"Rico was in great form last night, wasn't he," she said, for something to say. What was it Bella wanted?

There was Bella. "Won't you sit down?" Julia spoke to her as if she were a stranger, or a vague acquaintance, a caller, in the old pre-war style. Bella was a caller. She had put on that frock for this occasion. Only an hour ago, going out to fill the jug, Julia had met Bella on the way to her room, in her usual coat and skirt. "You've changed your dress." There was no reason for Bella to put on that green silk, or was there?

"I wanted to talk to you," said Bella.

"We don't seem to have much chance to talk, do we, any of us, since the Fredericks blew in?"

"No."

"I haven't anything but tea," said Julia.

"I have some Vermouth upstairs," said Bella and before Julia could stop her, she was gone; she was back.

"Oh, what fun," said Julia. She went to the book-case and opened the cupboard where they kept their shoes and the dust-pan and various oddments. "I thought I had some glasses. Oh—here." She deliberately chose the Venetian goblets, not suitable for Vermouth, that she had kept so carefully shoved away, hidden at the parties. "I have these goblets, not exactly suitable, but pour in a little Vermouth, as if it was old brandy."

Bella poured in too much.

"That's too much."

They sat facing one another across the big table that Julia had been so carefully clearing up before Bella came in.

"You keep hearing from Rafe?"

"Why—yes—why yes, Bella. Why?"

"Well," said Bella, turning the stem of the Venetian goblet—"why—"

"That glass matches your dress. It's—it's old glass—well, not so old, but Venetian; there's a superstition, isn't there, that Venetian glass lasts as long as friendship? I mean, that is if two people get Venetian glass—that their friendship lasts as long as the glass—I've been very careful of these glasses."

"I never saw them," said Bella. She did not say "You got them with Rafe." She must have known that.

"I got them with Rafe," said Julia, not letting this moment pass. "I'm glad you came in, Bella." She went to the cupboard, she found another glass. "Let's leave this for Rafe."

There were three glasses on the table.

"I want to say," said Bella, "that—that—Rafe is coming back, soon."

"Yes," said Julia

Bella said, "You know, I never really care very much for people." She spoke defiantly, "I had a lot of lovers."

"Did that matter?"

"I mean—I never broke across a man and his wife. I did not mean to break across a man and his wife."

Well—what was there to say?

"This Vermouth reminds me of Rome. We always had

a glass before lunch—they told us if we had a dash of quinine in it, it would keep off malaria."

"Yes," said Bella.

Julia saw Bella almost as if for the first time. Her expression did not change. Her colour would not; it was patently and prettily put on, out of a box. Rico had giggled over that with Elsa; "She has different shades" Rico had said, after exploring Bella's dressing-table. During the day, Bella kept her little room and Elsa and Frederick were down here.

"It's rather crowded. Elsa tells me they will be seeing Molly Croft to-night. He thinks they may be going to that cottage in a few days."

"But—" said Bella.

"But what?"

"Elsa told me that you and Rico—"

Oh, so Elsa had told her. What else had Elsa told her?

"I thought it was understood," said Bella, "I thought you would be going up to my room at night. I was surprised the first night, when you stayed here." How tell Bella?

She said, "Well—no, I mean, it's difficult. I was here alone with Rico that afternoon when you and Elsa came in, after shopping. He didn't say anything about it."

"Well, Elsa said you had been writing, that it was all arranged. I thought that you and Rico—"

So she thought that I and Rico.

Rico had said that Bella was suffering from suppressed hysteria. There was that about Bella. She sat very quiet, her wild-rose tint, her hair combed tight back and varnished, her dark eyes pulled up at the corners were a mask; her words were rather toneless, that sort of American toneless intonation, running on one rail, unlike the great swoop and sweep of Elsa's singing German voice or Rico's curious dynamically stressed utterance or Rafe's somewhat over-sauve quality that made every word he uttered poetry. Bella spoke in a voice that went with her marionette make-up. But she was too taut, she was simmering inside; if she once screamed—Oh, God—don't let her scream. But why should she?

Julia said, "Things have been very difficult for everybody—" How could she tell Bella what Rafe had said, what Rafe kept writing, "It's only to forget—I want to be with Bella when I am there. I think of you here."

That was his last letter, all of his letters. But of course Rafe being Rafe might write the very opposite to Bella, with that hyacinth-myrrh poetry he had been sending her. Julia knew about the poetry, a love-and-war sequence, because Rafe had left copies of the last lot with her; "Read them," he had said, "they're written for Bella." Everybody was so damned outspoken. There was a catch somewhere.

Now Bella was being outspoken. Why couldn't she keep to her odalisque rôle, with her tight-pulled dark eyes and those two hairpins stuck in at the back of her long bob which she had screwed up into a tight knot with those pins, stuck in at a perfect marionette angle, making her look like Madame Butterfly. Well, someone had to be Butterfly. Certainly Bella in her green silk, her rose-paint, her insect black up-darting eyebrows, her simmering narrow dark eyes, was perfectly in character. But Bella was not all "character."

"She is suffering from suppressed hysteria," said Rico.

"Cigarette?" questioned Julia quickly, before the doll

should break and its mechanical wheels and springs bounce out and roll about the carpet. "Everything's very difficult for everybody," said Julia, looking for the match-box.

Spontaneous combustion—whatever that was. It seemed that something of that sort might happen. Green chemical in a test-tube. Rico's chemical, the formula that was Rico, made itself felt; you knew when the formula Rico was at work in a test-tube, this room. It left a trail in the dull grey or clouded heavy atmosphere or it sent out sputtering spit-fire like a cat spitting. Bella was chemical, she was simmering underneath. Rico was right about the suppressed hysteria. She was so very quiet. Oriental she looked with those tilted eyes and the green frock and the eye-brows strained upward and neatly pencilled like the antennae of an insect. Butterfly?

She was beetle with a hard shell, her green silk might have been plate metal. She seemed metallic, as she sat there, refusing the cigarette, now lifting her glass, setting it down, and tilting Vermouth into the goblet. She moved with set precision, as if she knew her part very well, but was having stage-fright.

Why should she be afraid of me? Does she expect me to flare out at her, at this moment? Why, no. Bella is Bella. Someone had to come into their lives; it was nicely timed, Ivan in Petrograd and the little room empty upstairs and Bella and her mother flooded out of their flat in Paris. At least, that was Bella's story. Why not believe it? They were all suspect. Julia herself was actually housing a German, Rico was in wrong with the authorities, they were all outcast. Bella must say something or she would burst; Rico was right, something was boiling away but far underneath, suppressed hysteria.

"My mother is a modern woman," why yes, yes. They had met Mrs Carter in the old days when they were here in London, on the way to Paris; Ivan had introduced them. Mrs Carter was a journalist, well dressed, living from hand to mouth. She had put Bella through an art-school. Mrs Carter was apt to fly off at a tangent, her constant preoccupation, "I believe in women doing what they like. I believe in the modern woman." In 1913, the "modern woman" had no special place on the map, and to be "modern" in Mrs Carter's sense, after 1914, required some very specific handling. "I believe in intelligent women having experience" was then a very, very thin line to toe, a very, very frail wire to do a tight-rope act on.

With her white hair, her eighteenth-century carefully preserved complexion, Mrs Carter was, in a way, a valiant woman. But—but—the line was too thin, the demarcations remained what they always had been. There was the war and things that happened in the war. But later when Rico met Mrs Carter, he said, "It's a pity she gives the show away—" he scratched the back of his ear like a very fetching monkey, put forward his best French foot, salacious, worldly, "Madame Carr-rr-taire, entrepreneuse," he said.

"You tyrannize his soul," said Bella.

The Vermouth was chasing gold flame, then (a sip) gold flame round an empty (her body) test-tube. This is the first drink I've had, thought Julia, since those last parties. Abstinence creates, it was spirit, a gold fire in her. She drained the last drop, set down the goblet. What did any of this matter? The Vermouth was herb, crushed dandelion, she thought. She was reminded of the Chartreuse she and Rafe had sampled at the monastery outside Fiesole—was it? Bella should know.

"Where is it they make this stuff—or Chartreuse?" she said.

It took a very little to go to her head. Her head was lighted with amber flame, just this drop of Vermouth. Bella tilted the bottle toward her glass.

"No more—why don't you smoke?" The grey smoke of the cigarette was added incense.

"I don't care very much for smoking—you tyrannize his soul," said Bella all in the same breath, as if she were bent on speaking her lines, this particular set of words, she flung out, tonelessly.

Bella might have been saying anything, it's a cold evening, or do you believe in ghosts? Ghosts? They were visibly about her, Rafe on the Appian Way, a cypress in the graveyard where they laid a wreath of pink and white alternate camellias on Shelley's grave. They fell from those trees. Rose-red, rose-white. She and Bella were opposites, oriental, nordic. No wonder Rafe was so very sure about it, they were completely different. It was all so very simple. Now Bella was putting out a claw, cat-claw, black panther. Rafe was coming back soon and Bella had something to say about it.

"I can't stand it," said Bella in her toneless one-tone voice, as if she were speaking lines, not very well stressed, lines she had learned, knew perfectly. There was a catch somewhere. Bella was not just surface-Bella, green beetle, encased. The beetle-wings were fluttering, the beetle-claws were unfurling. The insect had a scorpion sting, or had it? Something's got to be done about it this time.

That is what Julia had kept on repeating but when Rafe blew in with his "This is the last time, I won't come back, there won't be a next time, you might let me have my fun with Bella, it's the last time, it helps me to forget," there wasn't anything to do about it.

"He isn't there," said Bella, "you tyrannize his soul. When he's with me, he's thinking of you," said Bella.

There was Bella telling her something in a toneless, one-tone voice and it was rather horrible. Why must Bella tell me this now?

"You see," said Bella, "I wouldn't have had any money, how would I educate ut?" She said "ut", Julia noticed, sensitive as she was in her over-fastidious way, to vowel sounds. "Ut?" Who was this "ut"? "Ut" was the child that Bella might have had with someone in Paris, and really this was the last straw.

There had been so many last straws, the camel's back was broken, it was dust and dried bones in the desert. There wasn't any camel for any last straw but Bella was saying, "You see I might have had ut," as if all this time (how long ago was it that Bella had had that operation?) she had been brooding. Yes, brooding, like an animal, gazelle. Some brooding deer-like animal had been hurt, horribly and it was all the same to her; she shrugged the green silk shoulders, poured herself another glass of Vermouth. "After all," she said, "I suppose I didn't want ut; I mean," she said, "how could I have educated ut?" As if she were wanting confirmation from Julia, wanting Julia to say, "Yes, of course, it's all right, you were very sensible."

Julia said, "Well—tell me—" and Bella went on, in her one-tone slightly drunken (but she was not drunk, was she?) toneless voice.

"It was horrible. The woman said come back, it's too early—then she said, it's too late—" then Bella went to another woman. But this was dreadful. Bella had been slashed about by unauthorized abortionists—are any ever authorized?

"You have to be very careful," said Julia as if she were an authority on the subject, "of course, in Paris, it's easier to do these things."

My God—was Bella telling Julia or about to tell Julia, that it was happening again?

"I really wanted to have a child," said Bella. Was she drunk? Was she pretending? "There was Paulette in the quartier; she had a child, its father was killed before the next permission." Quartier, permission, they were in another world now. Did Bella think that Rafe was going to be killed? Did she want or was she having, his child?

"You're not—there's nothing—?" Julia managed to articulate.

"Sometimes it seems to me as if nothing was real, as if all that in Paris had happened in a dream," said Bella.

Bella said, "After the battle of the taxis—we all followed —they laid them on the pavement—the boy—" What boy? A boy in horizon-blue, an American fighting for France?

Shall I ask if he was that boy—the father—what does Bella want me to ask? She had arrived in London very chic, with patent-leather suit-case and a round hat-box and a travelling-rug like someone travelling in a play, got-up, made-up, Paris, London. Bella was doing fashion notes for a New York-Paris journal. But Paris fashion notes were not what Paris fashion notes had been. But there was Bella doing her bit for civilization: cuffs are worn longer, the new fichu. There was Bella in the exact ultra-fashion of last war-spring.

The room, the books, the table, the two little gilt chairs, the rug on the floor, these things were comparatively secure, compared with Bella. Bella had been left by the tide, the worse war-tide of Paris had washed up Bella, foreign exotic, bright parrot, a bird that talked, that was uttering toneless words, as if those words were utterance put into its head from outside, parrot-talk, it didn't mean anything.

It didn't mean anything, what she was saying, that she wanted to have a child.

Did a parrot like Bella, writing notes on frills want—want —What was it Bella wanted? Did any one of them know what any of them wanted? They were all marking time. Rafe was simply another lover, young officer on leave, *permission* Bella called it, and *I have a rendez-vous with death* was the singular leit-motif of what Bella was saying; she was not living any more than the rest of them were, in any known dimension. Maybe Bella was drunk. It was the first time that Julia had seen her narrow eyes widen, had seen tears in those eyes.

Bella cried prettily. The tears spilled down her rose-tint and did not spoil the prettily put-on rose paint from the rouge box upstairs. What was it Rico called it, not apple-blossom? No, *fleur-de-pêche* he said, exaggerating his French as if he were proffering a box across a counter in a beauty shop. He put Bella on the map with his *fleur-de-pêche* and calling her mother *entrepreneuse*. But there was more to it than just that. Rico made neat pictures, put Bella on a band-box, painted her on a fan. But opening the fan, there were other dimensions, layers of poison-gas, the sound of shrapnel, the motto that ran across the top of the fan when it was spread open was *I have a rendez-vous with death*. Bella had known that boy, too, in Paris.

He had gone, and the other in horizon-blue, who came here to see her, would go, probably; what other still? Bella was seeing this, in those terms. Rafe was just another officer on leave, *permission* she called it. Soon, he would be back. But this apparently was the first complication that Bella hadn't banked on.

"There was never anyone like him," said Bella, and she was talking of Rafe Ashton now, apparently, "He doesn't really love me. He isn't there. When he is with me, he is thinking of you." This sounded damn familiar, this was simply herself, this was Julia talking, this is what Julia herself had said, or thought rather, having no one to whom she could possibly say it, about Bella.

"You tyrannize his soul," said Bella; "he loves my body, but he isn't all there, half of him is somewhere else."

How could Julia tell Bella, that exactly the same thing happened in her case? She told Bella, "But it's the same with me. I never feel he is thinking of me now. It's almost better when he's not with me."

"Yes," said Bella, "he loves my body but you tyrannize his soul—it's you he cares for."

The funny thing was that facing Bella, Julia felt that she was looking at herself in a mirror, another self, another dimension but nevertheless herself. Rafe had brought them together; really they had nothing in common. They had everything in common. At any rate, Bella was making a straight statement. You knew where you were with Bella. She looked vampire-ish, the stage type of mistress, but no. She was eighteenth-century in that frock, she was something out of a play. They all were. Certainly she was right, this couldn't go on, it could not go on for ever. "I thought I might move out" didn't solve anything. "Did you tell Rafe?" "Yes—no." Anyhow, what did it matter what Bella said now, the thing would matter only when Rafe was there to face it. It was Rafe's problem. "It's Rafe's problem." "Well, he doesn't face anything. He says wait till the war is over." Did they all say that? She and Bella were simply abstractions, were women of the period, were WOMAN of the period, the same one. But this thing couldn't go on. Bella was shot to pieces, with nothing to show for it, but her patent-leather hat-box, her bright fringed shawl, her two tortoiseshell hairpins stuck in, à la Butterfly. Rafe was simply another young officer on leave. Did they all act like this? "Well—Bella—"

What was there to say to Bella? They couldn't sit there talking all night. "Suppose we leave it to Rafe, suppose we wait till he comes back." Would he come back?

VII

But this was nonsense. Now she saw that it was nonsense. The show was rowdy. Things were all out of shape. The house should be bombed to hell or the house should stay still. The house was supernaturally still. There would be this pause, then there would be the tic-tic-tic again that people said, that Miss Ames and Mrs Barnett (the secretary at the War Office) upstairs, said were "our guns." What did it matter whose guns they were? "They're trying for Euston again," said Miss Ames, "such poor shots."

Yes, they were trying for Euston, trying to smash the railway communications and they were such damn bad shots that they spilled their stuff round Bloomsbury, Queen's Square, Mecklenburgh Square; "Not even hitting the British Museum" said Miss Ames, indicating with her cigarette-holder the unseen but frightfully heard Prussian airforce, "It's lucky isn't it, that they're such bad shots."

That was the answer to the last lump of dynamite they

had unloaded. "Won't you wait downstairs, Mrs Ashton?" But Julia excused herself, politely, "I'll go upstairs, if you don't mind." "Be careful of your shutters, we don't want any more official enquiries," said Miss Ames, her parting shot. But Frederick and Elsa had gone now; they had Molly Crofts' little house in Hampstead.

Rat-tat-tat began again. The room did not shake. The books did not fall down. It can't be such a bad raid. Now there was no question of pretending anything was the same, would ever be the same. Martha was quiet and discreet, the munition girls greeted her politely on the stairs as usual. But now everything was different. At least, everything was exactly the same, but so much worse, like the centre of a cyclone. The centre of a cyclone is still. So she was. There was the table, the book-case, her constant inventory. But looking at table, at book-case, taking inventory, she gauged, as it were, the strength of the storm without, by the behaviour of the objects within, like watching small articles in a stateroom in a ship in a storm.

Certainly the room was quiet. But more than that; she herself had been centralised, had found a focus. She had told Miss Ames that she would go upstairs, she expected to be alone. But she was not alone. She was not surprised to hear a tap at the door. People always climbed up, one of the munition girls or Mrs Barnett or Miss Ames to see if she had changed her mind, wanted after all to join them in the downstairs living-room or even in the basement. But this was not Miss Ames. It was Vanio, the young man whom Frederick had brought to parties.

This was the young man who was to have been Elsa's partner. But things worked out differently, she and Rico had not been intimate as Elsa had expected. But some law of emotional dynamics drew Julia and Vane together.

He said, "I told you I was coming to take you out to dinner."

"Yes, yes," said Julia, "you did say you were coming."

"Did you forget?"

This was ridiculous. Didn't he know there was an air-raid?

"But the air-raid."

"Oh—that—" he drawled, in that curiously attractive manner, "I didn't notice."

"Sit down—won't you—" She sank back in her chair. There was the other chair, where Rico had sat. Rafe's chair. He sat down opposite her, in Rafe's arm-chair.

"Do you mind if I smoke?"

She did not move, she waved to the marble mantelpiece, then motioned toward the table. "I don't know where the cigarettes have got to." But he pulled out a pipe, he stuffed a pipe with tobacco. He struck a match. He had always been sitting there. Someone was always sitting there.

"How did you get in?"

"Get in?" He looked up, quizzical. His eyes without his glasses were screwed half-shut as if to focus. They were slightly tilted at the corners, slate-grey. Screwed half-shut, his eyes had a quizzical contemplative look, they assessed her. "Get in? I walked in the door, as usual."

"Was the door open?"

"Someone barged in."

She did not ask who this was, it might have been Bella or even Mrs Carter. Julia did not want to talk of Bella, nor of Mrs Carter.

"Well, it's odd you came in. I went downstairs to get my bearings. Miss Ames was in the hall and she wanted me to stay down there, do you want to go down there?"

His slightly screwed-shut eyes had a look of half-quizzical amusement. "Wh-y?" he questioned making two syllables of that word, making of it ironic comment on the whole show.

The rat-tat-tat took up its old game, where it had left off.

"I don't think Miss Ames would like us to go out. She considers herself personally responsible for everyone in this house. Could we go out?"

He did not answer, for the rat-tat-tat was receiving a little volley, a little salute, a little response, an answer, a slight dump of dynamite, not so far off.

"We might wait," he said, with his supercilious slight drawl, "if you don't mind, till I finish my pipe."

She slipped on her coat. "We must creep down in the dark," she said, "there're no curtains at the hall windows." She switched off her own light, opened the door. The hall lay dark, like the hall of a haunted house, the Georgian window at the turn of the stairs gave shadow-light that became clearer as they stood there. There was no sound inside. Standing at the head of the stairs, she was herself now playing her own part in this curious mixed partners, dance of death? dance of life? Suddenly, it was a game, after all. They had turned out the lights. They were playing hide-and-seek after a party, this was after a party. In the chance blind-man's-bluff, she had inadvertently, blindly, grabbed a partner. The partner loomed tall and ghost-like at her shoulder. His hand was on the banister.

"Shall I go first, Person?"

"Why, no. I know the stairs better. Just slide along after me."

They slipped down the stairs, playing a game in a darkened house. "I don't think anyone will come out. I think they're all in Miss Ames' room, I don't think they're in the basement." They crept past the door like children playing a game; her hand was on the front-door knob. "Slide after me and if Miss Ames pops out, we'll run."

City of dreadful night, city of dreadful night. She saw the railed-in square, the desolation of the empty street. It was a city of the dead. There were no lights visible in the blocks of walls that surrounded them, iron balconies gave on to the square and the plane-trees stood stark metal. They lifted metallic branches to a near sky that loomed now with a sudden spit of fire. A volcano was erupting. Along streets empty of life, there were pathetic evidences of life that had once been, an ash-tin, a fluttering scrap of newspaper, a cat creeping stealthily, seeking for stray provender. Ashes and death; it was the city of dreadful night, it was a dead city.

A branch lay at her feet, blown or broken. It was a branch of a plane-tree.

"Don't get tangled in that dead branch," she said, remembering his near-sightedness, "there's a branch blown down or broken." But he stepped aside, pulling her with him as another spurt of fire and brimstone told them that the war was not yet over. Silhouette of uneven chimney-pots and irregular roofs was cut out of cardboard. A sudden clang very near, then swift diminuendo, an ambulance. She was going out to dinner, she was dining out. They started back against the iron railing. She felt the iron of the rails run furrows through her coat, as she registered a final nerve-shock. That one was quite near.

"They're going now," he said. "They can't get any nearer."

. . . clinging to an iron rail, clinging to a dead branch, she was saved. But the branch was not dead. Maybe, it was the very branch she had followed with her eyes, that day seated on the chintz couch, the other side of the room, when Frederick had been over there by the fireplace, writing. The branch made her think of Rico. Maybe, it was the very branch, cut neatly off by a bit of shrapnel, maybe it was a dead winter-branch blown down. A branch, anyhow. There at her feet, was a branch. Here at her side was someone come to help her. It was Rico who had brought Vane to the house. It was Rico who had been *maître de cérémonie* at those last wild parties. It was Rico who had helped her.

It was Rico who had jeered "You and Vane are made for one another."

It hadn't worked out as Elsa, as Rico had planned, but it had worked out. Inwardly, she saw the room, the other side of the square. She could turn and peer across the square, could see the house. Was the house still standing? The house was there. It would loom large in imagination, it was a wall about to fall upon her. But she had escaped, she had got out of the room, she had got away from four walls about to crush her.

"I'm glad we got out," she said.

She saw the room far off, then looming near, like a ship at sea, pushing on at them, looming up, about to ride over them. But jerking herself alert, she found she was standing on a pavement. There was no war. Everything was quiet.

Vane was quiet. But he would say something. Something would be said. Something would be settled. Now for this moment, there was the uttermost static peace, the centre of the cyclone. Round her, all those emotional events were projected, but far out. They were dancing this dance of death, in this supernaturally quiet square.

There was Rico, saying "We'll do a charade; you be the tree of life, Julia."

Adam and Eve were Rafe and Bella of course, Vane was the angel at the gate. It was the end of madness. It was the beginning. Vane was the angel, a joke with an umbrella. "Take your umbrella," shouted Rico, "Vanio, you be the angel with the flaming sword," and they had screamed as Vane had posed with the umbrella, static and calm, the angel at the gate.

"Dance," said Rico, "you dance," he said to Julia.

"But I'm the tree," she said, "or what am I?"

"You are the apple-tree," said Rico, "you dance. Now Adam and Eve, you come along here and Elsa, you be the serpent," he said, "you growl and writhe."

"Serpents don't growl," said Elsa. But she obligingly

plumped herself flat on the floor and wriggled on the blue carpet. They had shoved aside the table. There they all were, and Captain Ned Trent screamed from the day-bed, "What can I be, old Rico?"

"You be the audience, you be chorus of the damned; come on, Eve."

Eve snatched a branch of laurel from the jar by the Spanish screen.

"Excellent, Bella, come along, Rafe."

"What are you?" said Rafe, "what's left for you? Oh, I see, old Rico of course is Gawd-a'-mighty."

Rico took up a Jehovah-like pose by the fire-place; he chanted from an imaginary scroll, "Women, I say unto thee. . . ."

"But that's not Jehovah, get back to Genesis," shouted Rafe.

"Well, dance anyhow," said Rico, "the Tree has got to dance; dance, hand them the apples," and the chorus of the damned shouted from the day-bed while Elsa writhed her Teutonic serpent pattern on the carpet.

It was very quiet. Vane said, "We can make a dash for it now, or would you rather go back?"

"Go back?" She felt symbolically clear, frozen, static, standing there by the rail. She realised that her bare hands were clutching the cold rail. She unfastened her fingers as if they belonged to someone else; fingers had been frozen to an iron rail. She felt in the pockets of her loose coat. "I forgot my gloves."

"You want to go back?"

"Oh no, I mean—I forgot my gloves, my hands must be

filthy with this iron rail." She rubbed her hand in the darkness against her coat. "No. I don't want to go back," she said, "I don't want to sit in that room."

In her head was a picture, seen at the far end of the field-glass, very clear; tiny figures unfolded in bright colour. Bella was in her green frock. Rafe snatched a laurel-branch to match hers. Rico was standing; Jehovah. Captain Ned Trent was sitting up on the edge of the day-bed.

"That's the best Bible-ballet we've had yet."

"Yet?" asked Julia, "what else have we had?"

"Oh, it's all day of judgment," said Captain Ned Trent.

"You're not any judge," said Rico, "you howl, you howl with Elsa, you're the chorus of the damned, complete with serpent."

Julia swirled round them, offering apples.

Now suddenly a curtain dropped. She saw, drawn rather badly, an out-dated stage-scene, scene for a background, walls drawn in crude grey and black, black spaces that were black blank walls; a door opened.

"I think people are beginning to come to," she breathed, "a door opened."

"What?" said Vane, leaning nearer.

"This show, this particular show is over." She pulled herself, by an effort, from the iron rails. She felt as if she were glued there or held there by some magnetic force. She staggered toward the curb, tangled her foot in the branch. She thought of the etched branch outside the window where she had sat, the other side of the room, while Rico went on writing. Rico would go on writing. She disentangled her ankle from the branch. It's not a dead branch. Golden bough. She thought of the branches that Rafe and Bella had plundered from the jar in the corner, at Christmas-time for Adam and Eve. She thought of herself dancing.

"Those red spots on your cheeks, is anything wrong?" What did he mean, is there anything wrong?

"Why—no—it's the excitement, it's this wine, I suppose."

"But you haven't touched your wine yet," he said. She lifted the goblet. An amber light was reflected from the goblet. Around her, there were voices, clatter of dinner service. The small room was crowded. There was a hectic atmosphere, people laughing and ordering more wine—many officers. There always were. Vane looked at home here as he looked at home seated in the big room. Here they were, as they had been in the big room, as they had been at the parties. This was a party. There was an unusual amount of shouting across tables, shouting at the waiter. It was the aftermath of another air-raid, they were all safe. They were collected in this small crowded upstairs room in an expensive restaurant, like people who had known each other a long time. Waiters were deferential. Vane looked like a young officer on sick-leave with his stooping shoulders, his aristocratic languor.

She held the goblet in her two hands. She felt the gold pouring into her fingers from grapes and sun. These grapes were grown on another continent, another world, before there had been war, the warmth of past suns warmed her cold hands.

She lifted the goblet. A new idea came to her, something

about gold grapes and the porches of Cos. Yes, it must be Cos.

"What are you thinking, Person?"

"I'm thinking of islands, of an island—"

"Yes," he said, "you must come with me to Cornwall."

He had said this before. He had said, "When the war is over, you must give the Captain a fresh chance." Then he had said, "You can't stay here another leave of the Captain's, it's suicide." It would be suicide, she now decided, to stay one more leave of the Captain's. But she would stay just one more leave (would there be just one more?) and clear up the situation, that would never be cleared up. She felt prophetically that the situation would never be cleared up; but she said, "I'd like to wait just one more leave; then if things aren't any—different, I will come."

"I want to know," he said, "I can't go back there alone to that empty house. Ballentyne keeps writing me to join him in Ireland."

"Do you want to go to Ireland?"

"No," he said, "I want to stay in Cornwall."

He said, "I want two things, I want to finish my opera and I want a beautiful relationship with a woman." He had said this before. She would go to Cornwall.

She said, "I will come to Cornwall. Only, I want to stay one more leave. I told Rafe I would be here when he got back."

Nobody was to blame for anything, or the war was to blame for everything. This was the new note, the new dimension, this was not-war. This was Vane, a young musician, who did not talk of war. This was another set to be reckoned with or rather something from the outside to pull her away from the old crowd. There was Ballentyne in Ireland; there was de Meroff, a young Russian in the censor's office, whom Vane had had in, a friend too of Rico's. Those were people, only indirectly concerned with this war. She would go away.

It was not Bella's fault.

It was upsetting, Mrs Carter was in town again. Maybe Mrs Carter was taking charge of Bella. Bella isn't my charge, Ivan left her with me, but what right had Ivan to do that? Ivan in Petrograd was actually responsible. If it had not been for Ivan, Bella would not have come. But I could not have gone on, anyway. It was not Rafe's fault.

"It was not Rafe's fault."

"What, Person?"

"I was only thinking out loud. It's nobody's fault."

She saw that her glass was empty, she saw Vane tilting the narrow pre-war Rhineland bottle toward her. She remembered Bella and that bottle of Vermouth and of how she had said to Bella, "We'll let Rafe decide." But that leave (the last) there was no deciding anything. Things went on faster and faster, but then things had not come to a head; even then, she had still felt that Rafe was expecting too much of her; even then, oddly, he had been her husband. Things had gone round and round (was this room going round? This is only my second glass) and the end came, when she no longer felt anything. That was a strange moment, almost a new cosmos had rayed out from her, feeling nothing as she stood in the door, as she stepped forward into a room.

"Rafe, I met Miss Ames on the stairs, she asked me

where you were—and Bella—" That had been the last human experience and thank God for that.

Something went still in her and she knew they were there on the other side of the room, actually in bed together.

It was true, quite, quite true that Julia had asked Bella to be careful, had said don't risk going up to your room if the munition girls are around. She had meant it but had not meant it as literally as all this. But she must have meant it. What difference did it make whether Bella and Rafe were upstairs in Ivan's little bed-room or whether they were downstairs in her bed.

"You must be careful," she had said to Bella, "if there's any danger, you better take the big room." So—she had been out with Morgan—she found them in the big room. There was no need to explain. She explained it from the darkened door-way.

"I didn't expect to get back so soon, we couldn't get into a theatre. But I met Miss Ames on the stairs and she wanted to know where you were." Drag husband, mistress out of your own bed, "We better go downstairs, I'm sorry—" sorry?—"but Miss Ames was rather snappy." She did not switch on the light again. She waited. "I'm sorry."

No. She had felt nothing at all. She had felt nothing at all.

"What are you looking at?"

"Oh—I—I'm not looking at anything," she said. But this was not true. She was looking at something.

"You look funny," said Vane, "don't you feel well?" He was thinking of her, asking her if she felt—funny.

"Funny," she said, "why no."

He said, "I thought you looked as if you had a touch of fever—" he was thinking of her.

Julia saw the room. This is not my room, this is an upstairs room in an expensive restaurant. She saw the crowded tables, the waiter was pouring wine, setting down an ice-pail.

"No. I'm all right. Maybe, it's this wine."

"You haven't had much," he said.

"No. But it's a good deal. I mean it's good wine." Now the room was this room and her room dissolved into the smoke of countless cigarettes of other officers on leave. All the other officers were the same, they were the same shape. They all wore brown belts. They wore, she supposed wrist-watches. They all thought alike. They were so many paper-dolls, a string of paper-dolls, a hundred, a thousand officers on leave.

"I told Rafe I'd wait till his next leave," she said.

"You told me," he said.

The palms of her hands cupped the crystal goblet. She held solid crystal in her hand. A shifting plane of gold that had been Rhineland grapes steadied her, concentrated her, held her to her centre. Cyclone-centre, she had thought. But to achieve the very centre, it had been necessary for a million young men to die. It had been necessary . . . but don't think. There they all are, shouting, and now that group swaying to Tipperary

"It's getting very hot, don't you think we better go now?" for she could not endure the thought of even the very least of these young men going back . . . going back . . .

But this was madness. This was touch of fever. Impossible to live so intensely, keyed-in to all this. They're happy, aren't they? Well, let me be happy with the same sort of desperation.

She placed the goblet carefully back on the table. Yes, the room was going round. No, she was not drunk. Or was ... two glasses ... yes, it was obvious that she had a touch of fever.

Yes, she must get out. Yes, she must go home. How convey to him that he had helped her, healed her? For surely she was helped, healed? A goblet, two goblets, a few intimate words, the vista of sea, gulls, rocks, the house he spoke of. It was haunted, he said. But haunted with something different, far ghosts, not real near ghosts, men who might be ghosts to-morrow, the latest vintage (1917) grapes to be crushed ... There they all were. But she was already cast out, trodden under foot, she already had died. Already she was out of her body, she patronised them in her tolerance. She had escaped, was dead, they had that yet to do.

They would be going back to-morrow, this morning. She would be going back ... back to a room that was tomb ... or womb that had ejected her. There she was standing against the door, she had just closed. There was the darkness. There she felt, knew. But she did not quite know, she had not yet switched on the light.

"I'm sorry," she heard herself say.

"Rico is funny."
"What did you say—old Frederico?"
"I was just thinking," she said, "of Rico, of how he said

to me you are *here*, Elsa is *there*. It's all so neat with Rico. But it isn't. Yet it is. Somehow it didn't work out that way, but you are *here*—" She did not say what she was thinking, feeling.

She could not so grandly gesticulate toward eternity, as Rico; "for all eternity" was a long time. But somehow it had worked out. Vane was *there*.

"I think you were right. I think I may be going to have a touch of fever. I mean—it's all this—excitement—and the room—and this wine—" He was propelling her toward a door, through a crowd of tables. The cold mist of the London night was the same cold mist, dark, as when they had come in. But outside now was the hectic aftermath, the streets crowded and a group shouting. He would get a taxi. Vane was the sort of person who would somehow always manage to get a taxi. It was that manner. It was his detachment, his air of indifference, the feudal hallmarks. Perfectly, he was there to help her.

"You're too tired to go to the pictures?" he said. Pictures? He was offering her pictures, he was offering another dimension, the actual black and white of screen-projection. But he was offering her other things to look at, vista of blue sea, gulls. Pictures? It would be better to go anywhere than back to that room. It would be her own fault now, if this thing were spoiled. She was the only person who could spoil it. She must be like Rico; "You are *there*," she should say constantly to herself, "yes, there, there." She reached out her hand and found his, a large firm hand yet sensitive, perceptive. "You are *there*," she said aloud, laughing, "you are *there*." Yes, he was there.

It would be madness to reject this gift, this gift of the

gods, of Rico. It was Rico who had brought him to the house and it was Rico ironically who had precipitated this, contrary to any original idea, the animals go in two by two. "You and Vane are made for one another," Rico had jeered. And even if they were not exactly the-animals-go-in-two-by-two, they were both projected out, they were singularly aloof, alone. Even if they were not the human animals going two by two, yet they were two separate entities who had found each other, "the Tree of Life," as Rico had called her, and "the Angel at the Gate," as he had labelled Vane.

They had not the simplicity of the original-sin of the original and one and only, Bella-Rafe number. Bella and Rafe were the original human elements, Adam and Eve, and Rico was Gawd-a'-mighty as Rafe called him and poor Elsa, by law of contrasts, had to be the serpent. God and the Serpent, Adam and Eve, they were all neatly mated, and what better than to pair off the Tree of Life and the Angel at the Gate? She found herself laughing. Yes, it was very funny.

"Why are you laughing, Person?" He leaned toward her, his shoulders were wide in his great-coat, but thin like an Egyptian's. His eyes peered forward in the gloom of the jolting taxi.

"I can't help remembering," she choked, "it's all so dreadfully funny; do you remember old Rico being God at the party?"

"God?" said Vane.

"Oh, don't, don't say you don't remember."

"Oh," he said, "*that* party—"

"Yes and Elsa, the serpent, poor dear Elsa, he would give her that part and you—and—me—" She stopped laughing.

"I'm not—not—drunk—or—anything. I mean, I can't help thinking how funny it is," she said. "Here in this taxi is the Tree of Life and the Angel at the Gate, *for all eternity*," she said.

It was all very clear now. What was going on outside, was going on outside. It had nothing to do with her. There they sat centralised, the Tree and the Angel, *revenants*.

The pit beneath them was filled with smoke of countless cigarettes that wafted a cosmic brew, a sort of narcotic dope of forgetfulness. They were seated at an awkward angle in the corner of a box, the only seats left in the house. She was glad to be there. If they had not been able to get in, something else might have happened, she might not have decided, might not have managed to say finally, "But of course I'm coming, write your housekeeper, make arrangements." She had made, or was about to make a gesture. If she said she could not go to Cornwall, Vane said he would write Mrs Farrer, his housekeeper to shut up the house, come back to town. He could not, he assured her, stay there alone, now that Frederick and Elsa had gone.

She was edged in the corner of the box. They peered down on the screen, they were too near and too high. They were not good seats, but the last in the house and it had been necessary for some reason to come here. To-night, something was decided. As she peered over the edge of a box, she was looking down on the screen. She had been summoned or invited or propelled toward this box, this seat in the circle.

Below her, below them, were the thousands; it seemed that all the soldiers in the world, symbolically were packed

into this theatre. There was music, too near, pouring at
them from an organ, playing the usual sentimental ditties
and the voices of the thousand thousands of all the soldiers
in the world were joining in to swell this chorus, this Day
of Judgment; how many of them would come back?

The Angel at the Gate peered indifferently, "I'm sorry
you're so perched, Person." "I like it," she said.

They peered over the edge of the box and a foreshort-
ened car dashed round a sunlit cliff, and adjusting to the
angle, she realised that the silver wavering was the very
shape and texture of olive-leaves, flickering in the wind.

Oddly, it was not America, there was the usual mountain
slope, hairpin bend, but it was Italy. The car swept on. She
was dragged forward with the car and the voices rose up in
rhythm to the inevitable. The car would swerve, would turn,
it swerved, it turned, they swerved, they turned with it, it
was dashing to destruction along the edge of a narrow cliff,
they were dashing with it. But no, good-bye Leicester
Square, the car swept on. She edged forward further, her
eyes were adjusting, focussing to this scene of danger with-
out. It was danger without. Inside she was clear, the old
Greek katharsis was at work here, as in the stone-ledged
theatre benches of fifth-century Greece; so here, a thousand
doomed, the dead were watching destruction, Oedipus or
Orestes in a slim car, dashing to destruction.

Good-bye Piccadilly. No, it swerved, it bent, they
swerved, they bent with it. The multitude, herself, Vanio,
all of them swerved and turned. She was part of this. She
swerved and veered with a thousand men in khaki, toward

destruction, *to the sweetest girl I know*. But no. A swift turn, a sudden slide of scenery, a landslide of scenery projected the car, its unknown mysterious driver onto a smooth road. He was rushing along a level road, such a road as lines the waterways outside Venice, on the way to Ravenna. Was he rushing to Ravenna? Where was this? It was outside, anyway. *Good-bye Piccadilly, good-bye Leicester Square.* They were all rushing toward some known goal. The car veered, jerked, turned in at a gate—slanting, gigantic, foreshortened below her line of vision. He had come home.

He was let in. He had to be let in. Striding with hero-boots toward a door at the end of a seemingly endless corridor, he was yet striding toward some known goal, some known objective. It was not yet. But soon there would be some unravelling of this mystery, *it's a long way to go*.

This was the answer to everything, then, Beauty, for surprisingly, a goddess-woman stepped forward. She released from the screen the first (to Julia) intimation of screen-beauty. Screen? This was a veil, curiously embroidered, the veil before the temple.

The garden was tapestried in quatrocento leaves and flat flowers. The flowers were large (magnified under a glass) in her hands, Persephone in Enna. She turned and a wind caught the fluttering stuff of her scarf. She twisted it suddenly round her head. Now she was a hooded woman, Demeter, looking out. She was watching from the rocks (Primavera with her flowers) the flight of another car, rounding the same bends, in tangible perspective.

Now as she runs back to the house, the screen darkens,

she peers through a window; outside, rain twists the branches of palm-trees. A stone-pine stands immovable through the tempest. Ghost-wind, a ghost banging of a casement-window is seen, not heard while the cinema-organ breaks into operatic aria. Love-motive. She is watching for the first young man—the hero?—while another—the enemy?—rounds the same curves, projects himself forward toward the same inevitable screen-destruction. This time, surely, this unknown but exactly apprehended "other" must dash off, rounding the last terrific hairpin bend, to inevitable destruction. But not yet.

The Greek messenger will convey all that, presently, entering with ghost-gesture, indicating with ghost-gesture, the solution of the mystery. Not yet.

She climbs marble stairs out of a fairy-tale. She is a mermaid, trailing along marble stairs, clinging to a marble banister, while screen light and shadow flow over her. She emerges; drowning, she staggers toward her mirror. Pushing back the wet stuff of the palpably mermaid garment she regards the face, the same face from a mirror. Venus and the looking-glass, Persephone in Enna, Primavera.

There are violets in the air.

Softly, to the tune of out-moded aria, she pushes back the dark hair from the white forehead, and as the screen veers to show her reflected image at still closer range, one sees the flower-scattered rain-drops on her face. The camera swerves, the flower-tears have vanished and she lifts, as if in replica, to replace them, a diadem of brilliants.

There she was exactly incorporated, no screen-image. Here was Beauty, a ghost but Beauty. Beauty was not dead. It emerged unexpectedly in the midst of this frantic maelstrom. The Spirit moved, gestured. The smoke from the thousand cigarettes was incense, breathed by ghosts-to-be, toward Beauty. Julia was part of this, part of the teeming crowded theatre, one of the audience, one with them, *good-bye Leicester Square. It's a long, long way.*

But not too long, not unattainable.

"Take me away." She was standing. The theatre lights switched on at the interval, showed the thousand uncovered heads, all alike, smoothed back, here and there a white arm in a sling. For the most part, the arms in slings wore khaki bandages. That is what she saw.

She was gazing into a charnel-house, into the pit of inferno. "Our languid lily of virtue nods perilously near the pit." The old-fashioned theatre curtain now mercifully swept to the floor. Heavy dusty maroon velvet had mercifully slid across the veil of the temple, where just a moment since, a miracle of light and shadow had embroidered in luminous threads the garment of a goddess. A palace, a temple, an olive-tree. A palm-tree, a stone-pine, a flagged-walk through a garden. A spray of wild wet narcissus, Venus in the looking-glass. A circle, a diadem of brilliants, the northern crown, *aurora borealis*, dawn, a new dawn, a star-dawn had been demonstrated.

Julia stood on unsteady cramped legs, her back to the pit of inferno.

She saw a dusty box-curtain with looped tasselled cords, like a curtain in a Victorian doll's-house. "We might as well go." The voices rose again from the pit, voices of heroic angels, surging on toward their destruction, *pack all your troubles in your old kit bag and smile, smile, smile.*

VIII

The room was cold, cold, the blue curtains still fell to the floor in dignified long folds. There were books on the shelves. She seldom took out a book now. There was the table, carefully dusted. There was a little cluster of winter-hyacinths, in a kitchen-tumbler, on the occasional table at her elbow.

She had only to wait. It was very quiet, waiting. What went on upstairs was none of her affair. She did not even know if Rafe had gone away, if he were still there. He was still here.

She waited as if nothing had happened. She had seen the old Rafe (a ghost) here, heard his voice, she did not have to read the Madrigals. Everything had been quiet, yes, she had seen them going out, heard them come in, but the burning in her head was almost gone, she had Vane to talk to. She wore the blue corduroy-velvet that fell, they said, like Parthenon folds, its corduroy-velvet lines giving, they had said, a Greek line. Very cold, very old, as old, much older than the Parthenon, she stood by the marble mantelpiece. She stood, as Frederick had written, by her frozen altars, very cold, very old. There had been pipes on the mantelpiece; why, there was still that old briar. She did not take in the fact that Rafe Ashton had come in, for he had been there, off and on, whether he were in England or in France, and she never knew, anyhow, if he were dead.

The flowers he laid on the carefully dusted, unnaturally neat table with its books piled painfully neatly, were daffodils. She did not know if this were a dream or if this was Rafe Ashton come back. It was Rafe Ashton come back.

She stood like someone in a play, she would have to say something, she was very cold, very far away, very frozen by her frozen altars.

Whatever he said would make no streak and spark, fireworks in this room. The fireworks had sizzled out, the show was over. The chemicals in the test-tube had done their job. They had projected her out, the same, different, the same, a little clearer, a little harder, a little (to quote Rico) more dangerously frozen. All that had been for this—that she herself should simply be where she had been in the beginning.

He was metaphorically booted and spurred. His greatcoat was over his arm. He was evidently going to the station. Of course, Bella was going with him. Bella might burst in now, or even Mrs Carter. Julia said nothing, for Mrs Carter or Bella might come in. They were always with him. Well, that had been part of her bargain, that last talk she had had with Bella, before Christmas. She had said (had Bella told him?) "Let Rafe decide." Well, he had decided.

Julia had brought no pressure to bear. She had asked simply that they be more careful, "Come in here if Miss Ames is upstairs," she had said and Bella had taken her literally. She had not actually meant, go to bed in my bed. But Bella was logical. Rafe? They had slept there in that bed. Well, that bed was that bed and she had not slept in it since, with or without Rafe. All that was long ago. She remembered how they had searched London for just that low wide couch that would look all right in the daytime with its cushions, that would not make a bedroom of their living-room. But this room was part of a house, those three long windows. It made them part of a house, this room. There was the bathroom upstairs and their old furniture was stacked in the cellar. What would he do with the old furniture? She certainly wouldn't want it.

"I want to thank you for all this. I realise what you have done for me," said Rafe Ashton.

He wanted to thank her for something and her head was very cool. She could listen to his words. They left no spark and trail in the air. Little bits of Pompeian marble, a jutting-up edge of wall opposite Trajan's column in the Forum, the deep well where someone leapt, where there were those hordes of stray cats. Rome, that was. The glory that was, the grandeur that was. The words he said brought no scent of orange-blossom blowing from Sorrento across the Bay of Naples. A goat-herd fluted no high note; *bid me to live and I will live* was just a song put to music out of the Elizabethan book of madrigals, somewhere over there on that shelf. She had sorted and arranged the books. She would be going away. Not to-day, not to-morrow. She would go over her papers, she would have to search out some clothes. She had not thought of clothes, for a long time.

Would Bella go on with her designs? Or what? Well, what would happen to Bella? Mrs Carter had worked it all out or hadn't she? Was Mrs Carter worried? In any case, it is no longer my affair, my responsibility, thought Julia. I put it up to Bella or Bella put a pistol to my head with her "all or nothing" and Rafe with his "I will go mad, I am torn in two" and so on. Well, he would not go mad, he was not torn in two. He was one person. She had left him alone. It's for Rafe, she had told Bella, to decide. She had stuck to her end of the bargain. Well, Rafe Ashton had decided.

He put his hat down on his great-coat. He had laid down his great-coat on the little gilt chair, first looking around to see where he could put it, like a visitor. He was a visitor. He placed his hat on top of the great-coat. He looked round the room.

He would never see her in this room again. What happened to the books, would be his own affair. She would take one or two small things she had brought from America, those little apostle spoons. There was nothing she wanted really. He had laid the daffodils on the table. Let them lie on the table. *That come before the swallow dares.* Those Wordsworth daffodils of *the inward eye of solitude* are frost-bitten, she had written, long ago, sitting by that table. He need not write any more.

"You need not write any more."

"What—what—Julie?" said Rafe Ashton.

"I was only saying that it won't be necessary any more, to write. All this must have been a burden to you." He was crossing the room. He was taking her hands. Whatever he said would mean nothing. The fireworks had sputtered out, in the icy blackness. "Why—Julie—"

He said, "Why, Julie, don't you realise that your letters mean everything to me? I left the last lot over there on top of the books for you to keep for me."

"Did you?"

"I came in one evening when you were out."

"Did you? I didn't find the letters." She saw now, on top of the books, on the lower left hand shelf, a bundle of the familiar grey-white envelopes. "I thought those were an old lot."

"You'll keep them for me?"

"Why yes. There was nothing in them."

She was still standing. He was going away. She did not care what he said. He could stay or not, he was a visitor, someone had come in to say good-bye. There was no flame and pulse in her head.

She had been crystallized out and the human throb and beat that had been her head, her heart, was quiet. The test-tube had done its job. The room was empty. Rafe Ashton looked round the room.

He was saying, but he was saying in a different way, "I won't come back." But whether he came back or not, she would not be here. "I told Vane I would try to go off with him to Cornwall, or rather I told him I would join him there, after you left. I wanted to see you, I wanted to tell you about it. There was so little time, I didn't want to worry you with details."

"Do you love Vane?"

"I don't think so."

"Does he love you?"

"I don't think so. We're just two people who seem to belong together. Like Bella and you."

But it was not the least like Bella and Rafe. It was something quite different, it was the other end of the sliding-scale or the other end of the thermometer or the other side of the map or the other side of the earth. All the lines ran parallel, it was the same thing, quite different, running in the same or the opposite direction, but with no blur, no fizz or fireworks in her head, not aftermath, not beginning, not end, something running in a straight line, a pattern.

"Why didn't you tell me sooner?"

"There was no time to tell you. I waited in, several evenings, but my head started burning again when I waited. I kept remembering, when I was alone in this room. I thought the best thing was to get out. You said you would go mad. Bella seemed to think that she—that she—well, she —I didn't know her mother was coming to stay upstairs. I told Bella I'd leave it to you. I didn't want to influence you. I left it to you."

"I see," said Rafe Ashton.

She did not look at the daffodils. They didn't mean anything. She looked at the daffodils. She said, "Thank you for the daffodils."

She looked at the daffodils. They were glowing spring-sun on the unnaturally neat table by the heap of neatly piled books.

He said, "I hope you will be happy."

"I don't expect to be happy." The words, as she spoke them, sounded acid, maybe bitter. She had not meant them to be. She did not mean them to be. "I mean—" but she did not want to tell him about that last bout of fever. These epidemics were getting worse in London.

None of this was in her letters to Rafe. She had wanted to help him to live, he said her letters helped him—what had she written? There was the last batch of letters, on top of the lower left hand row of books, over there on the book-case opposite. She did not want to hear anything more, to learn anything more. She had said to Bella, "Let Rafe decide." Is it possible he had not decided?

"I thought it was all taken for granted, I mean you said you would go mad, that you were torn in two. I thought, this way, you would be one person."

She said, "I thought you understood. I didn't want to worry you about it. It was not your fault. I couldn't help being as you said—well—paralysed—with fear—I mean, they told me at the nursing-home that I must not have another child—"

"Ah—" he said.

"—until after the war was over." The war will never be over.

He stepped forward. Like someone in a play. He took her hands. "Your hands were always so cool, Julia, I often think of your cool hands—like cold flowers." Civilisation was not dead, then, he called her hands cold flowers. "I can't go into this now. I want you to know," he said, "that you are the most beautiful woman in the whole world. Bella wants a child," he said in the same breath. "If it was just Bella and me, it wouldn't matter. It's something outside Bella and me." He called it a child. Bella had spoken of a child. Was Bella actually brave enough, did she know what she meant, did she know what she wanted? Or was it just the usual war-time trick, the harlot trick with soldiers? No, her thought made no such clear line of demarcation. No. She was not thinking like that.

He dragged her down to the arm of the big chair, he was covering her hand with kisses. "When the war is over—I want you to know—" But what was this he was saying? It had all been said a long time ago, over and over and over. He must go now. She did not want, did not dare allow any of that flame, that fire and acid seething in a test-tube, to get into her head again. Her head was quiet. Her head was calm. Her hands, he said, were cold flowers.

"Good-bye, Rafe. Thank you for the daffodils," she said.

She walked with him to the door, she watched him lift his overcoat as if it were a weight, a blanket. He took up his hat. He stood at attention, almost you might say, it was *rosenkavalier*, almost it was the old days when a young poet had been her lover.

"Good-bye, Rafe, I'll write you."

Now that everything was clear (Rafe had gone) and there was no problem but the immediate problem of life, the packing in a few days, Frederick came to see her. She had wanted Frederick and Elsa, had wanted to talk to them when she was worn out with grippe and fever. But now that she was well and Vane had renewed her courage and her strength, now that she no longer wanted nor needed Fred-

erico, Frederico sat beside her. He must have slipped in, as
he did in the old days when he stayed here. She had not
heard the bell ring; the knock on the door, she had thought,
was Miss Ames or Martha or one of the munition girls to
say, "I thought you'd like your letters, Mrs Ashton." But it
was Frederico.

She did not get up. He knew this room. He flung down
his hat and shabby out-door coat, as if he were at home here.
He was at home here.

"I'll get tea in a minute."

He sat down. The room was dim, the white hyacinths
were fragrant in this cold room. He sat facing her. She did
not want to remember the day, that first day when he had
sat there writing. Now he wore conventional town clothes,
looked like a solicitor's clerk. But for his beard. Cut off his
beard and he would be a pale-faced clerk in an office or as
she had thought when he scribbled away that day, a school-
master, correcting exercises.

What had he come for? She could have filled in some
lonely days with Frederick during the last month, but he
had not been in. It is true he was out of town part of the
time, moving from Molly Croft's Hampstead House to the
Kent cottage, to suit her own convenience.

"Well, Rico?"

She had to fill up a gap. She was almost too tired to say
even that, even to say "Well, Rico." He was ashes and snow,
he was as tired as she was. All that flaming test-tube idea had
been cerebral *tour de force*. What did the poems matter?
They were so much fireworks, escape. And why all this es-
cape? Why this vaunted business of experience, of sex-emo-
tion and understanding that they made so much of? It might

be all right for men, but for women, any woman, there was a biological catch and taken at any angle, danger. You dried up and were an old maid, danger. You drifted into the affable *hausfrau*, danger. You let her rip and had operations in Paris (poor Bella), danger.

There was one loophole, one might be an artist. Then the danger met the danger, the woman was man-woman, the man was woman-man. But Frederico, for all his acceptance of her verses, had shouted his man-is-man, his woman-is-woman at her; his shrill peacock-cry sounded a love-cry, death-cry for their generation.

He was willing to die for what he believed, would die probably. But that was his problem. It was a man's problem, the man-artist. There was also the woman, not only the great mother-goddess that he worshipped, but the woman gifted as the man, with the same, with other problems. Each two people, making four people. As she and Rafe had been in the beginning.

There was only the problem of waiting. She would wait for Vane to go down, get settled in again, she would pack, she would buy a ticket. What problem was there? Rico was saying something that seemed unrelated, he was speaking, almost as if he were concerned. What was he thinking?

"You are really going to Cornwall?"

"Why, yes. Why, I thought it was understood, you brought Vane in, you said 'You and Vane are made for one another.'"

"Yes," he said.

He said, "Why don't you take our cottage? You see, everything is there. We did up some elderberry jam. There are some books." He was offering her his cottage. "It's not so very far from Vane's. He could come in every day to see you." What was all this? It was Rico who had stamped about, uttered his shrill peacock-cry, his death-cry, his man-is-man, his woman-is-woman.

Didn't he mean any of it?

"It would make a difference," he said, "don't you realise?"

His face was white, all that sun washed off in London fog and mist. He was correct, almost puritanical. Julia wondered if he hadn't meant what he said—or meant it in another dimension. When it came to the actual fact of her going down to Cornwall, to stay in Vane's house, he seemed surprised, shocked even. She did not understand this.

She had not seen him actually alone, since that day here, when she had walked as in a trance, across the room to him, when he had shivered back from her hand on his coat.

It was the last time she had reached out her hand to him.

Now he was sitting there, frail and white in the dim room, with the hyacinths spilling their winter-fragrance.

The first time she met him was during the first days of the war. In a fabulous suite of rooms overlooking Green Park on Piccadilly. They discussed him before he came in. Someone heard he was tubercular, was that true? He had run away with someone's wife, a baroness, was that true? His novel was already being spoken of as over-sexed (sex-mania), was that true? A damn shame if they suppress it. Then the little man came in, looking slender and frail in evening dress that Rafe said made him look like a private soldier of the already-pre-war days, in mufti. Elsa was elegant, poured into a black gown. Her hair was like wheat. She was already-pre-war Germania. A symbolic figure. They had come back from Italy, summoned by a personal friend in high places.

Seated opposite her, now that the room was so quiet, was this same fabulous little enigma. The second time she had seen him was almost a year later, after she had lost her child. He suddenly appeared at her door, when she was alone in her Hampstead flat, in a smock, she remembered, peeling apples in that Spanish pottery bowl. "Come in. I think Rafe will be back soon." They hardly spoke. He watched her peeling apples.

Then here, just that one afternoon, after they came up from Cornwall. About four times alone, in all. This time. He was looking at her. This was the person who had watched her, not speaking, alone in the flat in Hampstead, peeling apples. He had not said anything about her child. He knew all about that. He was the only one who had known.

He knew all about everything. They need never speak. Yet here he was, I must say something.

"I'll put on the kettle."

"Do you realise," he said, "what you are doing?"

"Why—yes, I am going away with Vane. Or he is going first. I want to go over the books, pack."

"But—but—do you *realise?*"

What did he mean? She simply did not understand him.

He had written about love, about her frozen altars; "Kick over your tiresome house of life," he had said, he had jeered, "frozen lily of virtue," he had said, "our languid lily of virtue nods perilously near the pit," he had written, "come away where the angels come down to earth"; "crucible" he had called her, "burning slightly blue of flame";

"love-adept" he had written, "you are a living spirit in a living spirit city."

They were words, written in clear Spenserian, engraved on a calling-card, copy for a copy-book. They were all clear enough, and others. The charade they had played here when he made her the apple-tree, the Tree of Life. The way they had sat that day, when they did not speak and she followed the line of the plane-branch, painted on a screen, outside the window. All that. The lump of lapis-lazuli that someone had given him, that he had given her one day, "Take this, do you want it?" "Isn't that what Lady Ottobourne gave you?" said Elsa. "Yes—I'm sick of the Ott, she bores me," he said, leaving the lump of lapis there on the table, where Julia had been sitting, writing.

All this. Things spoken. Things not spoken. They were all having relationships, or would have—Rafe and Bella. Elsa had said, "Yes, you and Frederico, that will leave me free for Vanio." But that hadn't worked out. There was no sense in it. Given normal civilised peace-time conditions of course, all this could never have happened, or it would have happened in sections, so that one could deal with one problem after another, in due sequence. "Kick over your tiresome house of life," he had said, he had repeated it. What did he mean, then?

None of this made sense. Or rather, she had no longer any part and parcel in it. That was over. She had said good-bye to Rafe. The daffodils were over there on the large table where Rico had set down the lump of lapis-lazuli, "I'm sick of the Ott, she bores me." Spitting like a wild-cat. Drawing away his arm when she had touched his sleeve that day when

Elsa and Bella had come back. He could have come in at any time, if he had been concerned about her. Why had he not come sooner, why (now that it was all clear, all that past insanity of Rafe-on-leave nicely sponged out) had he come? Why had he come at all? Or why hadn't he come sooner? She did not ask him.

Would he, like Rafe, ask her if she loved Vane? "You are made for one another," said Rico at a party. Changing partners, changing hands, dancing round, in a Bacchic orgy of war-time love and death. Love? Death? He had moved across the room, yes, they had been alone that first time too, separated the length of that great drawing-room, overlooking Green Park. There were Elsa, Rafe, Mary Dowell of Boston and her friend Mrs Potter. Mary had collected them, was editing an anthology, a fabulously rich and gifted woman from Boston. Taking the whole top floor of the Berkeley, with the corner balcony overlooking Green Park. The window had been open. It was early August. The war was not a week old. "Don't you know, don't you realise that this is poetry?" said Frederick, edging her away toward the far end of the room. He held the pages that she had brought Mary Dowell for her anthology.

"Don't you realise that this is poetry?"

The war was not yet a week old and the child that she was just bearing only a few weeks old. That child had been living, and Rico touched her, to use his own expression "on the quick"; almost already, in that few moments' contact, that child had been his child. It is true he cared, not speaking, when the child died.

She realised in a strange detached way, that he really cared. Tenderness. That was it, not flame and seething passion, the dark-god he spoke of. Or if a dark-god, then one truly, Dis of the under-world; those white hyacinths were death-flowers; he had called her Persephone. The flowers were there. He liked her flower poems. He had particularly liked the blue iris-poem, that day at the top of the Berkeley, overlooking Green Park. Matrix to jewel, he had flamed around her, he was red-hot lava; then somehow he seemed to have projected her out, so that she was cool, cold, seated there. He was burnt out too, and white, but there was no dark flame now, none of his dark-god, unless he were Dis of the under-world, the husband of Persephone. Yes, he was her husband.

Herself projected out in death, was that dead child actually. He had been part of that, meeting him just as she was beginning to realise that it had happened. It happened actually almost identically with the breaking out of the war. Well, the war.

"Don't you realise," he said now, "that this—" he spoke quietly—he was not spitting like a wild-cat. He was burnt out, Dis, Death. "This—" he said, and didn't say anything. "I am not happy about this," he said, and he was Christ in a Flemish gallery, with his beard burnt to ash. He was painted on a canvas, now he was utterly himself with her. Not for the first time—perhaps there had been four times altogether. That time at the top of the Berkeley, then alone in her flat in Hampstead, then here that day and now. "You realise that," he said quietly.

There were many things to say, there was nothing. Nothing anyhow could now be changed. Something had been arranged. Rico had not altogether done this. Yet he had been agent, almost he had been medium, a medium. Something had to come of this, of this war. There was a knock. "I suppose that's Vane," she said, not moving, "he said he would be in." When she called "Come in," Vane came in. "Here's Rico. I was just putting on the kettle," she said.

IX

The wind was cold. Salt tasted. She tasted salt. Her lungs drank in mist and salt-mist. Under her feet was a new fragrance. She stooped to short ragged new leaf. She pinched a ragged tansy-like small leaf. It grew close to the ground. She lifted it to her nostrils. New fragrance.

She walked along a path in a drawing-book. It was a symbolic drawing, over-emphasized. A large grey boulder was half-covered with ivy, like a monument. Stark grey stones stood up. There was an actual Druid circle on the hill, Frederick had written.

He had written that the old path beyond Rosigran was made by the Phoenician donkeys that took tin from the mines to the ships.

There was a disused mine shaft at the edge of the road, across the space of grass and stones before Rosigran.

Rosigran, when she turned, stood like a house in a drawing-book or a house drawn symmetrically by a child on a slate. The roof was put on, like a roof that would come off, a house of a set of toy houses that children put together on the floor. To her right, as she faced the house, from the crest of the stony hill, lay the village where Rico and Elsa had lived.

The whole place was out of the world, a country of rock and steep cliff and sea-gulls. She sat down on a flat rock and wondered if the asymmetrical set of stones, just as the hill dipped, was the Druid sun-circle Rico wrote of. She found she was still clutching the weed-like leaf. She thought, "It's like something in a kitchen-garden." She tied it in her handkerchief. "I will send this to Rico and ask him what it is."

She got up, shook out twigs and last year's brambles from the edge of her skirt. She started down the hill. Then she stopped and gathered fresh ragged leaves of the same plant. She thought, "It's curled like parsley." There was a patch of ghost-flowers in some burnt-down underbrush. The skeleton twigs made a dead dwarf-forest for the carpet of ghost-flowers. They were wood anemones that fluttered and bent in the wind. Mist lay over the field of anemones and the twisted burnt twigs left from last year, like a dwarf-forest.

She followed a wall, following a trail of ivy. It was a huge trunk when she found it, the ivy was a tree really, that had trained itself to this wall. The ivy, she thought, might be hundreds of years old. She had never seen an ivy-trunk as thick as a tree. Old ivy leaves and new delicate ivy green showed separate.

In the wall was another unfamiliar leaf, like a seed-pod, growing under water. It stuck parasitic white roots into the almost earthless cracks of the stones, a leaf of another age, growing under water. She drew out one of the stalks from the wall, then another. "This will just about fit into an envelope," she thought, thinking she would get Rico to name these for her. Vane didn't seem to know the names of these plants.

It was not England. Rico had said that. Cliff rose defined against this mist. She was glad of the mist. It drew curtain over the startling expanse of sea-line that had stunned her into sudden reality. The scene displayed, the first morning after her arrival, was so clear, so vibrant that it had for a moment struck her as, not so much a dream, but part of the series she had called magic lantern slides, when her memory back in town, had suddenly apprehended (not seen but so suddenly apprehended) the separate cypress-tree or ledge of island within her, yet seen projected on the Spanish screen, in too bright colour. So this.

The jagged line of cliff, the minute indentations, the blue water that moved far below, soundless from the height, were part of her.

If she thought of Rafe, it was with a sort of gratitude. If there was fire, it was burning clear in crystal. The sky was not unlike the spring sky of Italy. Now she was glad the whole bright rock-landscape was clouded, with this cold, healing mist, as if someone had breathed a cold, healing breath; the very Holy Spirit had breathed on this.

She was enclosed in crystal. She was perfectly at one with this land. Everything that had happened back in London had been bound to happen. It had been necessary. Those who had precipitated its happening were each separately blessed by her. She wanted to lay flowers on an altar.

She had the same feeling that she had had in Capri, her word would call any Spirit to her, but she must be careful how she spoke. How she thought, even. It would be tempting something, luring something too poignantly near. She actually believed that if she broke a half dozen—or say seven sprays of those frail delicate anemones and laid them with certain words or thoughts even, on a flat rock, that something beyond this clear crystal (now this misted crystal) would be affected. That if she broke seven flower-stems, something would be altered.

She had walked out of a dream, the fog and fever, the constant threat from the air, the constant reminder of death and suffering (those soldiers in blue hospital uniform) into reality. This was real. She sat down on a rock. She unknotted her handkerchief and laid the stalk with the bulbous under-water leaves beside the leaves of the curled parsley-like plant. She re-knotted the handkerchief and placed it in her coat pocket. She was Medea of some blessed incarnation, a witch with power. A wise-woman. She was seer, see-er. She was at home in this land of subtle psychic reverberations, as she was at home in a book.

The very landscape was illustration in a book. The path she had just left, that twisted with apparent meaningless curves, was hieroglyph. It spelt something. Laid flat, unrolled, it would be a huge screen in a temple in Egypt. Then the path and the line of the cliff would be hieratic writing. She felt that every casual stone was laid here, there, for a reason. Phoenicians, Rico had written, made this track, and in making this track, they had trod into the soil more than the countless imprints of ancient sandals or thonged leather shoes.

Every breath she drew was charged with meaning. She drew deep cold mist, stinging, with the taste of salt, into her lungs. She was filled literally now with that divine Spirit, as remote, as beatified as a Yogi in a mountain temple. Snow, salt drifted. This fine mist fell almost in separate particles, like fine snow. The very white wild anemones were snowed there.

If her mind had lowered its vibration, its mood, to the mere mechanical act of thinking, she would have understood the symbolism of manna falling from heaven. She seemed to be fed actually by the mist that filled her body. The various irregularities of the earth-road, the stone path, the wall, the field with the thatch of dead twigs like a dwarf-forest, were vast in their implications, symbolic like a temple wall-painting, yet at the same time, they were sketched as minutely as a pattern on a leaf. One individual leaf, she might have philosophized, holds the soul of the forest, as one salt drop, the ocean's. So here, this walled-in space, was a world; the world, the whole world was given her in consciousness, she was see-er, "priestess," as Rico called her, wise-woman with her witch-ball, the world.

Beads of moisture settled on the sleeve of her old coat. Her coat was sanctified by it, this was another story of a fleece. Some parallel in myth suggested itself to her as she ran a bare hand over the rough grey woven texture of her old coat. She looked at the palm of her hand, wet now with

the condensed moisture, and even that seemed a sign. It
was a sign of something, she did not know what, did not
actually recall in her mind, a miraculous story of a fleece,
and dew in sunlight (was it?) fallen on it. Any fleece;
anyhow, golden.

They had talked of happiness. They had theorized of
sex-expression and experience. This was. This was the
deepest experience. All the same, if she had not so valiantly
attempted and so signally failed at their game, she would
not be here. If she had not condoned (she believed the word
was) Rafe's relationship with Bella, she would never have
touched bed-rock of desolation. Morgan had helped. They
seemed bent on demonstrating to her their sexual posses-
sions. She had felt like a child left out of a game; left out of
a game, a child crept slyly away to a corner of a large room,
found a book on a shelf. Opened a book. Another world.
Somewhere, somehow, she had been left out, Cinderella, to
dead ashes.

Somewhere, somehow, a pattern repeated itself, life ad-
vances in a spiral. She was not analysing herself in the new
mode of the Bloomsbury intellectuals, with half-baked mis-
applied theories from Vienna. She was feeling, however,
something explicit in this pattern. All this was meant to
happen. It was pre-ordained, written or carved on a temple
wall. She followed, had followed an explicit design. She had
not so much condoned Bella and Rafe as actually en-
couraged them, against her human, actual intention. But
over and above the human hurt, had hovered some other
non-human, abstract perception. Non-human? If the sex-
union they so vaunted was important, it was important to

them. To her? But in another direction or another mode, or another element. There was a game they played at children's parties, birds, beasts, fishes—what was it? This was not beasts so much as birds or fishes.

Chiefly, she was enclosed in the elements; a fish out of water (she had been too long in London), back in water, she swayed across the sea-floor. The mist above, around her was the sea-mist, sea. Each separate twig formed to her imagination, another genus; twig, stalk were twig, stalk of other un-named but racially remembered flora. Actually there were strange, unrecognised little stalks and bushes. She had never actually been in heather country, and here stalk and cluster of last year's heather and small tight bunches of heath were rock-plants from another continent. Another world. She had known gorse and broom, *plantagenet* in Italy. But here, gorse and broom and heath and heather and ivy and the un-named little stalk she had pulled from a crevice in the rock, were endowed with some special mystery. As if pronouncement had been put upon them and they actually held some sacramental power, left over from the days when actual Druid-priests had dragged those up-standing stones and formed a circle, small but of the same magical intention as the great stones piled at Stonehenge. Stonehenge? She was actually in a temple.

Under the sea. Like that sunken temple where it was reputed bells still sounded, not far beyond that cliff-head; Lyoness.

She flung her arms across her chest, hugging the old grey coat to her chest. It was cold. She was cold. Her hair hung on her cheeks in damp strands. She thought she must be looking very ugly. Her shoes were wet and heavy, caked with sandy earth. Real earth. Oh, the earth is real! Live things spring up here, even from the very dead old, old stones. Far away, she had left a toy-house, further away, a theatre.

Rafe Ashton in his uniform, was dressed up, play-acting, "That's the stuff to give the troops." It was all neat, all neatly dated, war-time heroics. Two women, three if you counted Elsa, but she was more like a huge *Dea ex machina*. It was a privilege to be able to contemplate such a huge, grand image, with straw-gold hair. And Rico, playing any part, but always, when he entered, taking for granted that his was the centre of the stage. His was the centre of the stage, however tiny the little act he put on, Miss Ames with her beads, or an Italian waiter or himself as a sort of prompter in the wings when they played charades at Christmas. Morgan, fey always, true to Celtic tradition, with her charm, her infidelities and her languor. Vane when he came there, fitting into some part already allotted to him, taking her away, out of that play, that trilogy, that room with the three French windows and the curtains. Little people coming in, one of the munition girls from the top floor with her letters, making a pointed entrance with a letter from France. Rico again, scribbling like an author in a play. Julia in a long blue corduroy frock that they said made her look like something from the Parthenon. Ivan Levsky before he went to Petrograd, still there in absence; they had talked about him; it was his room that had proved the turning point, his trip to Petrograd translating cables, had been responsible for bringing Bella to them. Mrs Carter taking the upstairs room when Mrs Barnett moved out, so as to give countenance to Bella, the last straw, "I believe in modern women." Molly

Croft as a voice off, offering Rico her cottage and the delay in getting it that had caused final disruptions. Other people, as chorus at the parties, Captain Ned Trent (he called himself an Irish rebel) who had run an ambulance in France. The boy in horizon-blue who didn't turn up after his permission (Bella's word) last Christmas. All the million in the background who didn't turn up. The sound of shrapnel. The noises . . . off. The tin-trumpet of the boy scout in the Square after the raid was over. Ironic nursery comment. The exits, the entrances. It was all minute, perfect as a play, her play. Bella in her green dress, in the grey fitted one with buttons down the front, in the ultra-fashionable one with the wide pleated collar that made her (she wore white make-up for that) a girl-clown in a ballet. Ballet? It was all ballet.

Far off (something she had left behind her) was the rumpled bed, the unwashed tea-cups, the ash-tray heaped with cigarette-ends.

She hugged her old coat tight, hugging herself tight, rejoicing in herself, butterfly in cocoon.

The wisps of hair grew damper, heavier on her cheeks. Admonition from childhood, "Don't sit on damp rocks," reminded her (and the thickening mist) that it was foolish to hug happiness on a wet stone. She did not know how long she had been gone, it might be two hours, it might be half an hour. The early spring was soft, fragrant, soaked with salt. There was a strange static quality, the ivy was cut out for a stencil, each leaf was separate and moisture settled, symmetrically like rain-drops in a pre-Raphaelite painting. The green showed like green in stained-glass and the yellow of the occasional early clusters of gorse-blossom was gold glass. Her perception was sharpened, yet she was not thinking. That tick-tick of her brain had been stilled, that pulse of fever in her, quieted. She stood up. Her feet, now she shook herself alert to this moment, were cold certainly. She moved swiftly down the exactly outlined path, where stones stood out, like a path in an Italian background. Each stone was shaped and rounded to some sort of inner perfection. How many years had this path existed? She was one with its druid asymmetry as she trudged toward the sea, realising that it was now late. The house loomed suddenly like a grey ship, rising from the sea.

The door itself, the grain of the wood, the green paint that edged the door-frame, the latch. A door. A simple door. This might have been barn, farm-house, abandoned inn. The lintel stone that lay flat was worn as stones before old inns or churches. She lifted the latch. She slid into a darkened space. The door swung behind her. She leaned against the inner side of the door, swung shut.

Her heart was beating, she must have run, that last bit. Her hands against the door felt stiff now; crucified or rescued on a raft, she was standing against the inner wooden platform that was a door set upright. Everything zoomed as if breakers were washing over a ship. The small window at the turn of the stairs, was square. The stairs had no banisters; ladder-like stairs turned squarely at the top. She saw the under-design of the four steps as the stair turned, like large pleats in wood. Such stairs could be folded from cut-out strips of paper (to set up in a doll's-house) or cardboard.

The table opposite held an old-fashioned oil-lamp with a china lampshade, such as she had cut out of the advertisement sections in the backs of magazines for her paper-doll house. It was the sort of lamp they place on a table, with a fringed shawl-cover, in a play of Chekhov.

There was a strip of fibre matting on the floor. To her right, as she faced the stairway, was the kitchen door. A hollow, under the space left by the upper stairs, held odd unrelated objects, a wooden box, a basket, a bundle of dried bracken-stalks for kindling. They were shadow outlines. To her left, was another of these doors with an old-fashioned wooden latch. The door was closed. It opened. A strip of light carpeted the hall, touched a highlight on the white china globe of the lamp from Chekhov. "You're late, Person."

"Am I? Yes, I suppose I am. I wanted to find that Druid circle, to write Rico, and I found some more stems, and leaves. I think he likes telling me their names. I ran the last bit."

Crucified against a door, rescued on a raft, she felt the light of the inner room broaden as he swung the door open. She saw the depth of the interior, the couch against that wall between the two windows, an edge of another window facing her, the length of the room. That vista was cut off, as he stepped down the one shallow step. "Where's Mrs Farrer? We must have tea."

"You're wet." She saw the top of his head, slightly burnished. His fair hair was sleek on the top, but an odd wisp or two stuck up, like a madman in the *Duchess of*

Malfi, with straw. He must be mad or he wouldn't have me here. She was blown into this door, the elements were with her. She would drip away to a pool of water on this hall floor, like some lady from the sea, fairy-tale, mermaid. She was so happy. She was so cold. She felt human continuity about to cut her off from the elements. I'm as wet as a sponge. She was glued to the inner side of the wooden door, like a door in a barn, an old inn or a church. He laid his hand on her coatsleeve. His face was in darkness. As he turned, she saw the oval of his face with the beak nose. He had left his glasses in the other room, on the table.

In a few days, she had learned his human peculiarities, as one may learn everything about a caged animal or bird, in a few hours. There was nothing wired-in, however, no cage; cave rather. The very wood of the door was part of the ancient grove, over the other side of the Druid circle that she had not yet had time to get to. The stone, the wood of this house were part of the rock outside, the cliff, the trees descended no doubt from some old Druid oak-circle. Everything was like that.

"I'll run upstairs," she said, "and change my shoes." Shoes, a wet skirt, hair that was wet suggested a towel on a towel-rack, a brush on a table. These things were separate, she seemed unfamiliar with them, yet fastidious. Fastidious like a lady from the sea, swum ashore, "I must tidy up, upstairs." Still his hand was on the wet sleeve, still the light showed dim profile, but race-old like these stones. His voice drawled, an affectedly aristocratic stoop to his shoulders, his slight ever so slightly weary, distinguished way of speaking. She listened to every word, marking as he uttered it, some special intonation. "Person," he drawled it slightly, it was always the same, always a little different. His ears were large, well shaped, set close to the oval dim face. He was conditioned like herself, to some special way of feeling. He felt as she did, more like a bird or a fish. Feeling everything, they did not need to discourse fluently on feeling. "You don't feel anything," said Rafe Ashton, and Frederick had spat at her, "Our languid lily of virtue." If she was languid, here was someone else languid, but what did they know of feeling?

Suddenly, her coat was a frozen pelt about her.

She felt her way, in the dim bedroom upstairs. It was not necessary to light a candle. She jerked open the second drawer of the heavy chest of drawers and fumbled about for the feel of stockings. Rolled in neat balls, shoved apart in the back left-hand corner. So far her eyes, her fingers helping, could distinguish, this is that old heather-mixture as they called it in that shop, almost pre-war quality, soft, carefully mended and cherished, long enough, stockings in England are long enough for me. She fastened one fresh, warm, soft stocking, felt the icy rim of her wet skirt, knife-cold against the other bare leg. "I'll have to shed this, too." She jerked off skirt and jumper, fumbled in the cupboard for something to put on, recognized the feel of the old blue corduroy. "I'll wear that." She felt for the dressing-table in the dark, brushed at damp hair.

She had left the door open. She turned at the head of the stairs. She looked into the pit of the hall, a stage with the Chekhov lamp now lighted. She walked into the lighted hall, stepped up the single shallow step, leading into the living-room; the door stood open, she walked into the room. Mrs Farrer was setting the teapot on the table.

"Where did you go, Person?"

"I don't know. Well, I mean, I climbed over the wall opposite the road where the road breaks off going toward St. Ives. It's all stones."

"Yes."

"But I wanted to explore; then I came back almost to the house again and struck up along the path that Rico wrote me about."

"The Phoenician donkey trail?"

"Yes. I just rambled along it. It seemed rather zig-zag and undefined but one always finds it. It seems to go on up over the top of the hill. I didn't go any further."

"It goes on after that, along some farm buildings, through a lane, and lands one, just this side of P-Z" (he called Penzance), "we must walk over one day."

"Yes," she said. "What did you do?"

"Oh, I pottered with some notes." Papers were spread out on his table, and ruled music-sheets. There was the piano, an old upright against the wall, then his table set in at the window, then the fireplace and the two armchairs, where they were sitting.

There was the pleasant crackle of firewood. Mrs Farrer paused in the door to ask if she should bring in more wood. "Just fill the basket," said Vane. He pushed his chair sideways to face the table, she got up and pulled up one of the stiff-backed small chairs and lifted the teapot. She filled the two cups. Mrs Farrer closed the door. The room was warm, bright now with the light of the hurricane-lamp that Vane said he and Elsa had chosen at an auction with some of the other things, the lamp in the hall, the set of plain chairs, this one, several upstairs and one in the kitchen. She had taken inventory of this house. Elsa and Frederick had helped Vane with the furniture.

He had had the bookshelves and his books sent from London, that couch, these two large chairs and the geometrical patterned strips of matting that were fastened up, along the wall, under the ceiling. They were a basket or wave-pattern, Javanese, he said. They were like the pattern on a Greek jar.

There were two windows, either side of the fireplace, one facing the door, and one symmetrically set in the wall-space opposite. There was his low chair before the writing table, that and this square centre table. On the mantelpiece, there was a tobacco-jar, a small modern statuette in bronze. There were the papers, pens, the usual collection on the writing table. The piano was piled with bound volumes of music and a few loose sheets. He must have brought the rugs from town, too. There was another set of smaller book-shelves, set in the space between the couch and the window, facing the door.

It would take her a long time to get over these last years, and here was space and time to do it. But specifically settled in this house, in this room, in this chair before the fire (Mrs Farrer had taken away the tea-things), she was conscious not so much of the war-years' wear and tear, as the reprieve this gave her. Wind from *Wuthering Heights* lifted a very visible dark wing from the sea, seemed to beat a great wing for some reason, with specific intent against the window at her elbow; the curtain billowed a little inward. The fire sputtered with some living force, the very branches were salt-soaked and dried in a strange sun. Salt seemed visibly to sputter, to burn with special chemical flame; a hard knot would reveal itself for a moment, outlined in a ring of fire, before the flame licked over and licked out the bent-branch outline. The branches were old gorse-bushes that Rico had helped him collect, he had told her. Was it Rico, Frederico, salamander spitting in that fire?

It was safe to think of Rico. The last time she had seen him was in a cold room, with white winter-hyacinths, a small cluster at her elbow. The Adam's fireplace with the scroll pattern was symbolic setting. She was tired of that graveyard. Rico had been right when he had gesticulated toward that grey sky in Hampstead and muttered his malediction, "It's grey, it's wet, it's like damp cardboard, it's like grey blotting-paper. Look—" flinging out his arm to demonstrate, "you stick your hand right through it." Symbolically, he was right. London had blotted her up, she was one of so many millions. London seemed inexhaustible in its power to soak up, to absorb. So much misery, so much indifference surrounded one, that one was almost left free, depersonalised. But London hadn't quite blotted her up (nor Rico) into its near sky, like grey blotting-paper. She was something else. Rico was a salamander in that fire. Here was an old, old parchment, everything here spelt something. Indoors as well as outdoors.

The wind, tangible, visible to the senses, shoved with a giant shoulder, there was a soft thud as if it were trying to push the house down. A gale? She rejoiced in it, wanted to shout back to it. A great entity, a visible Presence. It pounded on the wall, but nothing moved, no chair was displaced, books stood on shelves, the pile of bound volumes on the piano did not totter, the piano stood firm. It was wind, an inhuman element, a divine element. It did not play vile tricks, it did not shatter windows, it did not break nerves. Rather, it sustained the being of man, accustomed to battle with elements; man, woman could face wind pounding at a wall, find delight in it; through aeons, man had built firm against sea-wind, had conquered it. Long ago, this house would have slipped off the cliff edge, if man had not (long ago) discovered ways and means to fasten bolts, to weld beams, to fit doors, windows, against elements. Rico writing her, had been right, "Kick over your tiresome house of life."

This house was not tiresome, neither could it be kicked over. The wind pushed and made no impression on a stone wall, but the curtain flicked as if outside a finger coquetted with a petticoat.

"You didn't leave a light on upstairs?" said Vane.

"Of course not, I didn't have a light."

He got up. He selected a half-dozen volumes from the shelf. She did not want to read. But he was not offering her the books. He placed them carefully along the window-ledge.

"What are you doing? Can I help?"

"No—only—when this happens, pile up books, like this, against the curtain, will you?"

She had heard from Elsa of Vane's having been fined for showing a light on the sea side. She had forgotten all that. A coastguard would be at any minute passing.

The inhuman element might in its boisterousness betray them. It would not be forgotten that Vane and Frederick were friends.

"We don't want to be kicked out, like Rico."

"No," she said, "we don't want to be kicked out, like Rico."

X

She felt curiously that this room had been invented for her. It might have been said of her, from the moment of her entrance to this house, that she had felt the same of every room in this house. Every door, every shallow or steep step, every irregularity of passage-way, of door-sill held its peculiar and intimate reality. There was a charm over the house, of that she was now certain. This room particularly, perhaps, because from the first, even in the early days in London, Vane had particularized her status. "There are plenty of rooms," he said, "you can choose whatever room you want to work in." It had been implicit from the start. She was to have a room to work in.

The old house was partly unfurnished. There was an empty room beyond this. This room was wedged in below the roof, there was one small window. There was a small fireplace. Vane had had a table and a low rush-bottomed chair brought up. There was another low chair. On the chair beside the table was her open dictionary. On the table was her typewriter. The light fell over her shoulder.

The sun moving round the house cast its level light into this window in the morning. Beyond the window, was the framed picture; stones were piled in old pattern against the hill; on the slope, just out of sight, was the sun-circle. There was the shaft of the deserted tin mine, the wall. It was one picture, solid; the first level of stones on the hill were oddly symmetrical (to the right, over her determinedly turned back) like stones of a Greek amphitheatre. It was Greek in its implication, but archaic Greek.

The stones, the sun setting, rising, the ruin of the tin mine shaft, the trunk of solid ivy, all these would have words to describe them exactly in that Greek dictionary spread open on the low chair at her elbow. She was working on a chorus-sequence that she had always, it seemed, been working on. It would take her forever to get what she wanted, to hew and chisel those lines, to maintain or suggest some cold artistry. She was self-effacing in her attempt; she was flamboyantly ambitious.

The Greek words went with the texture of the stones here.

She was self-effacing in her attack on those Greek words, she was flamboyantly ambitious. The words themselves held inner words, she thought. If you look at a word long enough, this peculiar twist, its magic angle, would lead somewhere, like that Phoenician track, trod by the old traders. She was a trader in the gold, the old gold, the myrrh of the dead spirit. She was bargaining with each word.

She brooded over each word, as if to hatch it. Then she tried to forget each word, for "translations" enough existed and she was no scholar. She did not want to "know" Greek in that sense. She was like one blind, reading the texture of incised letters, rejoicing like one blind who knows an inner light, a reality that the outer eye cannot grasp. She was arrogant and she was intrinsically humble before this discovery. Her own.

Anyone can translate the meaning of the word. She wanted the shape, the feel of it, the character of it, as if it had been freshly minted. She felt that the old manner of approach was as toward hoarded treasure, but treasure that had passed through too many hands, had been too carefully assessed by the grammarians. She wanted to coin new words.

She pushed aside her typewriter and let her pencil and her notebook take her elsewhere.

It was none of it true, Rico. You were right about the frozen altars. But I thought if you wanted me, you would ask me to come up to your room. How could I climb those stairs, not knowing what you wanted? When I touched your sleeve, you shivered away. They seemed to think I was going up to your room, Bella's room that had been Ivan's.

I didn't think you wanted me, really. You said, next morning, you heard me singing in a dream and found your face wet with tears. Is that true? How could you say that casually, while Elsa washed the breakfast things behind the screen?

It couldn't be so casual.

Take away what I am trying to do, and there is nothing.

You can't light fire on an altar unless the altar is there. You are right about man-is-man, woman-is-woman, I am wrong. But it's no good. My work is nothing. But, Rico, I will go on and do it. I will carve my pattern on an altar because I've got to do it. You jeered at my making abstractions of people—graven images, you called them. You are right. Rafe is not the Marble Faun, not even a second-rate Dionysus. I wrote that cyclamen poem for him in Dorset, at Corfe Castle, where I wrote your Orpheus. But you are right. He is not Dionysus, you are not Orpheus. You are human people, Englishmen, madmen.

He is mad, too, this Vanio that you brought to see me. He wouldn't have asked me down here, if he hadn't been. But I am aware of your spider-feelers, I am not walking into your net. I am not answering your questions, "What room have you? What room has Vanio?" Not quite so obvious as "Do you sleep together?" I am not telling you of my reactions, or if there were or were not reactions on his part. A nice novel, eh Rico?

So Rico, your puppets do not always dance to your pipe. Why? Because there is another show. I don't in the least know what I'm saying. I left your letters with everything else in London. I did not have to bring them. I know them by heart. Why, in your interminable novels, do you not write—to someone, anyone—as you write me in your letters?

I am not sending this letter. I will find some more sprays and stems, practising, as you wrote it, my precious mysteries. Camomile-daisy, you said that first was, I called it tansy and the other I think you said was old-man's-beard or ladies-bed-straw or something of that sort. Then you stopped telling me their names. Why?

It was you who sent me here. I ask, "Where did that come from? Where did you get this?" to hear him say, "Oh, that was at P-Z with Rico."

He showed me the shop where you and Elsa chose the turkey-red for the kitchen curtains, those curtains that the coastguard reported. They cannot stop you signalling. You sent out a flare to me, that time in Dorset, before Rafe went.

Couldn't you have waited till he had gone?

Now she was shaken. "But why am I crying? I have never been happy like this, I have never felt like this." The cracks of the floor-boards drew off toward the door, too near for any actual effect in perspective but with eyes dimmed and half-shut, she was at her old trick, see-er, of seeing. The door was fastened under the slope of the roof. It was literally an attic, this small ledge of a room that she had chosen; it was her own, empty; the whole house was her own, all but empty.

There was a Devonshire jug over by the door, a jug placed there for an easy drawing-lesson, a Rembrandt effect, or a jug out of a Marriage of Cana sequence; when light this morning had struck under the low roof, it brought out the grain-pattern of the door, picked out the jug and left a sort of warm halo round it, as if the pottery jug were absorbing light, not giving out light, like a jar in the Marriage of Cana, touched with the aura of the miracle. It was all miracle.

Inside, was the jar, the candlestick, the basket or bushel, the loaf, the miraculous fish or her daily miraculous bread. Outside, were the two sparrows, and the countless unfamiliar birds that were already migrating from Egypt toward

the northern summer. They rested on this ledge (Vane had
told her) and the near Scilly Islands. "Why was I crying?"
she wondered. "I jumped off from a Greek sequence to write
something to Rico."

She did not want to re-read what she had written. Some
spring unwound in her, released tension. She did not want
to re-read what she had written. She thought, "I'll get some
fresh flowers for that jug."

Flagrantly creative, how could they endure you? Rafe
said, "There's Rico." You looked out of a window—off Bond
Street, it was. You had a hat on, a blue shirt, as I remember.
"My God," said Rafe, "who wants old shoes?" It was the
Medici print-shop. Has everyone told you, you are a dead
Dutchman, called van Gogh?

Now I am glad I don't know more about him. I have
seen enough, these few prints, a street somewhere—Arles?
I have seen old shoes, a rush-bottomed chair and a Devon-
shire pottery jug, filled with sunflowers. I have an idea that
the fields here were painted by a dead Dutchman, the shaft
of the deserted tin-mine, the dyke-walls. What were you
keeping out, Rico, when you built those stone walls? What
were you keeping in?

What became of the dead Dutchman? I know nothing
at all about him, just Rafe turning off Bond Street, "We'll
cut down here," and "My God, there's Rico" and "Who
wants old shoes?" and "Wait here, I'll chase that taxi."

How many Medici prints were there? Six maybe, the old
shoes, the sun-flowers, the road (Arles?), that cypress-tree

twisted in a whirlwind, the field at the second turning be-
fore Zennor, and the self-portrait.

It's all self-portrait. It's your inner self you're painting.
You made it all up, Elsa's work-bag on the floor, the cups
and saucers, the branch out of the window, when I thought
you were writing. You were writing or you were painting
rather, a branch out of the window, with the window-frame
one side and the folds of the blue curtain the other. You
drew the fanlight over the door, downstairs.

This house caused you no anxiety. It was easy to block
in, the whole thing was familiar. I, a familiar would be drawn
literally into your picture. How could I walk up those stairs?

I would be drawn, literally, up those stairs; would Bella's
room that had been Ivan's be suitable setting for a cypress
in a whirlwind?

I do remember what became of you. I think they locked
you up, in a mad-house at Arles.

And fortunately, there was Elsa. She could do without
non-essentials.

You see, I don't know what I'm writing and if I look
back as I did just now at that last sentence, I can't go on
writing. Why go on writing? I'm trying to explain to you
why I didn't climb up those stairs to your room.

I don't mean it was exactly Elsa. I don't know how to
put it. I don't mean exactly that you were her second English
husband and she had left the first and the three children to
run off (as they say) with you. You went to Italy. You came
back, warned of coming danger by someone in high places.
We were impressed with Elsa. We forgot she was a German.

I don't mean it's just because Elsa has been done out of

her country, her two countries, and her estimable first won't
let her see the children. It's something she has, forgoing
non-essentials. I forgo non-essentials or for-went them when
I didn't climb up those stairs. Granted, of course, that I
don't in the least know what I'm talking about.

There were certain phrases, I don't re-read your poetry,
but I remember somewhere (in Austria, I think) your writ-
ing of a terrace or a summer-garden by, or overhanging, or
overlooking a river. I don't remember anything about it but
the *gloire-de-Dijon* roses.

I don't know what that rose is; this is not a red rose nor
a white one, it is *gloire*, a pale gold. Not gold exactly, maize-
colour, pale corn-colour. It isn't a bit like Dante but then I
don't know Dante. It's Elsa's work-bag spilt on the floor.

I don't mean that stopped me coming up to your room.

Maybe it was Miss Kerr. You remember Mary Kerr's
novels, we talked about them—another of your spinsters.
Although she warned me off, at the end she couldn't help
herself. None of us could help ourselves. "Don't have any-
thing to do with them," she said, "there is a sort of *vendetta*
—not exactly a *vendetta* but the girl died. No, it wasn't as
simple as all that. Don't have anything to do with them,"
she said. She said the girl was teaching you Italian or you
were teaching her English, the daughter that is, of the
woman who looked after the place where you last were, in
Italy.

In my imagination, there was a summer-house, an arbour
and leaf-shadows on the written or unwritten pages of a
copy-book, like the copy-book you were writing in, that
first day.

I was told in St. John's Wood, in Miss Kerrs' drawing-room, not to have anything to do with you.

She could have left it at that but she forgot herself. "He knew the name of a tree in my garden," she said, "no one could ever tell me the name of that tree."

We should have left it at that.

"What did he tell you was the name of the tree in your garden?" I said.

"Key-of-heaven tree," she said.

Ridiculous, improbable, impossible. Did you make it up, the name of that tree?

Did you make up Miss Kerr telling me the story, with the signed Henry James above her writing-desk and the petunia curtains?

That is how it swirls round, so I understand your cypress —I mean the dead Dutchman's cypress—in a whirlwind.

It was all flat and I loved it, like pictures in a picture-book, every picture tells a story. Then it was no longer flat but went on in different dimensions. "We will go away," you wrote me to Corfe Castle, and the Raphael Tuck village street, the stone cottages, the postcard ruined Castle on the slope above the bridge, were no longer England. Or were they England?

Can England swirl round, re-born at the touch of Merlin?

XI

I will never see you again, Rico.

Vane said, "Have you written Rico lately?" He said, "You better write; the old fellow is very fond of you." But I told him to send my greetings in his letter. He said he was writing.

He is worried. They have sent him in fresh papers. Ballentyne keeps writing him to come to Ireland.

It no longer matters. Mrs Farrer is getting restless. He has told her she can get his flat ready in town, if she wants to leave here. She walks up and down the road, evenings, in her best black. Vane says she is too aristocratic to visit the farm people, as Elsa did. I go for the eggs sometimes. They are all kind and simple. Vane told Mrs Farrer that I was his sister. It is like that.

Don't think I am ungracious. We have the two top rooms, to the right, at the head of the stairs. Mrs Farrer moved from behind the kitchen into the other room. She doesn't like the knockers. I leave the door open between our

bedrooms. Vane had a sort of attack the last time we walked
back from Penzance. He lay on the downstairs couch, look-
ing like death. He said, "Don't let the Farrer come in." I
shut the door. I didn't know what to do. He said it was
nothing, "only that *tic*." You know his manner.

I suppose we will come back.

I started picking blackberries but there doesn't seem any
point now in doing up jam. We looked in the windows of
the Zennor cottage. They had taken down the curtains. The
blue and orange pillows looked "natural," Vane said, just
flung down, and the bookshelves "as usual." The door was
locked.

I don't think we have to come back immediately, but
the charm is broken. Vane said he would report at the office
in Penzance, "just to keep them quiet." I don't see the
papers but I hear from London of more "combing-out."
These words!

Don't think I am ungracious. I am only thinking toward
you.

I will never see you again.

I will go on scribbling. This very notebook is from the
Zennor post-office-stationery-cum-what-not corner shop.
You know it. This notebook is a replica of the one you were
writing in that day.

You wanted to know what I felt, what he felt. Well, I
didn't feel anything. I think his manner is defensive. We
play chess, evenings. There has been a good deal of gun-fire.
When I said, "What's that?" the other evening, he said,
"Only another ship. Your move, Person." He calls me
Person, *Personne*, Nobody. I wanted to get out, to stand on

the cliff-edge. I don't know what I wanted. But perhaps he was right. I absorbed so much misery in London—blotting-paper, you called the sky once. I think my psychic blotting-paper is all black. There is no room for more emotion.

Only this *idée fixe* that I want to thank you.

There would be no use writing you voluminous letters. I would be thinking, "What will he think," I would be feeling, foolishly, that I might be "material." I know that is stupid, self-conscious. You can write a book about us, if you want to write a book about us, without my help. But I think I wanted to help too, only I didn't want a sort of family album. I wanted a book to myself and as things are, the threads are too tangled. To write about me, you would have to write about Rafe—then Bella. I don't want Bella in it, not in our book.

I don't think I want Rafe in it, nor even Vanio.

You may think I am straining a point, if I say I want Elsa.

But I don't want Elsa, not as a person. When I "got out" in Corfe (I was in a fever) I went into a little house, quite a simple little house in the forest. You were out cutting wood, like a woodcutter in a fairy-tale. It was the air. I felt cooped-up in that cottage. I was writing the Orpheus sequence for you. But when I "got out" is was all very simple.

I was waiting for you.

I could sit on the porch-steps—do you say porch in England?

Perhaps it was America.

But not the America we know—but you don't know America.

I finally crawled downstairs. The county—can you be-
lieve it?—had been to call, that is, the Padre's-daughter-
cum-Doctor's-wife, friends of someone the Everyman peo-
ple had sent us to see, in Devon. They sent us because
Swinburne had stayed in that house and written—I can't
remember, one of his later un-Swinburnian long poems. It
was all deadly and dead, but they were so kind. The house
was a deserted palace and they had bushels of ripe peaches.
The Doctor climbed up to the room and left me a bottle
of invalid port. It was your letter on the breakfast tray that
had given me the fever. I couldn't tell him that.

When I finally went out again, the chalk hills were just
magic lantern slides.

That happened in London sometimes, in that room.
There were magic lantern slides projected on the Spanish
screen.

You started this.

Perhaps the port started me writing those poems to
Rafe. He was like that in the beginning, and we had been
to Italy. I could see him, a sort of vine-god, projected at the
foot of my bed. I thought then he wouldn't come back.
Well, he didn't come back.

Perhaps the vine, our youth dies in all of us. But I don't
think it does. He has, true to character, overdone things.
But I think he will come back. I mean, the young officer,
not the image that I saw there.

It wasn't a graven image.

It left me free.

Elsa said when you made your pronouncement by the

fireplace "It will leave me free for Vanio." But I don't think she really wanted Vanio. She would never be free.

I would be free if I could live in two dimensions. It didn't seem difficult in Corfe, and then he went to France. It was difficult in London and Vane was right when he said, "You can't stay here another leave of the Captain's, it will be suicide."

Captain?

It was "scrounging" he said, "wangling." But he helped drag out some officers, in a gas-attack. They were buried in a shelter. He was shouting it in his sleep. When I shook him awake and asked him, he said it was only because they were drunk and didn't hear the alarm. They sent him back for special training. But it doesn't matter, does it? The gas has gone from my lungs.

Perhaps I was afraid you had tuberculosis, though the rumour we first heard was contradicted. Or perhaps I was afraid just then, of having a child. But I wasn't afraid—that is why I was afraid. Do you see what I mean? I was walking into a new dimension. It couldn't mean anything but death.

But sleep-walkers, they say, don't fall off the roof.

Suppose I should wake up?

Once a Dakota poet I knew said systematic starvation was a sort of dope. I don't mean we starved actually. But doing without non-essentials leaves room, a room. I walked into it here.

I kept to my chorus-sequence. I would have another volume. I would get something out of this war. But what I got out of this war isn't a Greek chorus-sequence.

No doubt, I will finish the sequence and tidy up some of my old lyrics. No doubt, another slim volume will attract the usual very small but very discriminating public. But that isn't what I want, that isn't what I'm after. I want to explain how it is that the rose is neither red nor white, but a pale *gloire*.

It didn't suddenly burst open. I don't know when it happened. But when I think of Merlin, he is not an old man. Old man's beard? No, it was ladies-bed-straw and then you stopped writing me their names.

I thought I was someone but he calls me *Personne*, Nobody. I am nobody when it comes to writing novels. But I will find a new name. I will be someone. I will write these notes and re-write them till they come true. Maybe you haven't tuberculosis.

I don't mean the T.B. would make any difference to me. Only, I am susceptible, would catch something. I would catch your mannerisms, your style of writing, your style of thinking, even.

But that *gloire*. I must find words to tell you.

Perhaps I caught the *gloire* from you. Was it your way of thinking? But it isn't in your books, it was in your letters sometimes, when you weren't angry with me.

You might be angry with me. You might shrivel my hope. You might say I had no business writing of old shoes, ladies-bed-straw and the roots of the furze bushes you grubbed up and stacked under the stairs. There are still a few left.

Perhaps you would say I was trespassing, couldn't see both sides, as you said of my Orpheus. I could be Eurydice in character, you said, but woman-is-woman and I couldn't be both. The *gloire* is both.

No, that spoils it; it is both and neither. It is simply my-self sitting here, this time propped up in bed, scribbling in a notebook, with a candle at my elbow.

The child is the *gloire* before it is born. The circle of the candle on my notebook is the *gloire*, the story isn't born yet.

While I live in the unborn story, I am in the *gloire*.

I must keep it alive, myself living with it.

It is hard not to be able to tell you of this. I want to share this with you. You will think I could not face my ordeal, when you hear I have gone back.

It will be difficult to explain. I said I would never see him again in that room. I will not see him again, for I will not be there to see him. I will be living in these notes.

Miss Ames wrote that Bella and her mother had gone, that someone had lent them a house in Chelsea. I expect, Ned Trent. He was going back to France or Ireland again. I didn't try to follow. How could an Irish rebel be driving an ambulance in France?

Anyhow, they've gone.

It might as well be that room as anywhere.

The *gloire* is the candle at my elbow, but now the room is filled with sunlight. The couch is made up in the left-hand corner, under the slope of the roof beside the door. That is, beside the communicating door. It's shut now. The other door is open, it leads out onto the landing, down that one step. I sit with my back to the window. Everything is different since I moved here, that is since I left my first room. It isn't only that it's rather on top of Mrs Farrer, since she moved up, but it is before—before what?

It is before I left off working on the Greek, with the dictionary open on the chair.

It is before I started writing to you, that is writing in a notebook.

It is before I began to think of Vincent van Gogh.

Do you remember that picture, Vincent's room?

It isn't unlike this room, only this room is wider and has the couch instead of a proper bed, and this room doesn't really look like a bedroom, in the daytime.

I can't remember details of the picture, only the feel of it, clothes hung on a peg, those famous shoes (or the homely feel of them) somewhere.

Perhaps your room was something like that, in Zennor.

I imagined my Devonshire jug filled for the first time, with other flowers, zinnias or sunflowers. There are no zinnias or sunflowers here.

I had foxgloves, the last time.

I realised what you meant when you said my Coronal was made of flowers from the underworld, Persephone.

I had no sunflowers, zinnias or foxgloves in my first book of poems. You said you liked Coronal.

I saw that you were right and I hadn't come alive. I have left the Devonshire jug there, and the typewriter and the dictionary.

I did see, that first time, looking for the Druid circle,

how a path could make a pattern, letters, a sort of hiero-
glyph or picture-writing. But when I said I saw magic lantern
pictures, the pictures were all on one plane or parallel. They
were not dynamically exploding inside, like van Gogh pic-
tures.

I did make the great discovery that you looked like Vin-
cent and he became the person by the fireplace.

I could not explain my revulsion to your writing, nor why
it bored me. I am speaking of the bulky manuscript you
sent me to London, before I went to Corfe Castle. I did find
luminous phrases in your first books and the one they
suppressed. But I can't go into all that. I wanted to know
why.

Why what?

I wanted to know why I was overwhelmed and angry.
No, none of it was cheap. I can't explain it to you. Was I
jealous of your seemingly effortless expression?

I am not jealous of Vincent van Gogh. Then I remem-
bered Rafe saying, "There's Rico," and remembering that
Medici-print shop window, the dimensions came together.

The intensity that I strive for in my *Coronal* is a glass
slide in a lantern.

Just not striving gives Vincent's bedroom to me.

You go up the wide banister steps, along the corridor,
then you open the door into what might be a cupboard but
is the narrow enclosed flight of steps leading up to the top
floor. There was a kitchenette up there and two other rooms.
Ivan shared the kitchenette with the munition girls.

I climbed up there when Ivan was ill. He used to send me packages of Russian cigarettes when Rafe asked me to Corfe Castle, to be near his training-camp.

Ivan wrote me there, they had offered him the job translating cables. He was sailing almost at once. Would I mind if Bella Carter took his room? I did not mind at the time, I don't mind now.

I do not see the room with Bella in it. I see you rather, in Ivan's original setting, a bag of plums, a stack of old magazines and picture-folders, cigarettes and endless ashtrays. You don't smoke but there is a blue haze in the room. "Do you want more plums, Ivan, or shall I try for something else? How is your throat? No, I wasn't opening the window."

The window has a wide shelf, it suggests a dormer-window. Looking out, you see the sycamore or the plane-tree that I was looking at downstairs, but here, you are almost in the top branch. It was Ivan, now I think of it, told me that van Gogh was locked up. Now I remember, it was Ivan brought the folder down to my room.

It wasn't his, he had borrowed it, he was taking it back. He had a commission for a book on the Post-Impressionists but he couldn't finish it because of his censor's work at the postoffice, and then they asked him if he would go to Petrograd. They aren't anyway doing that sort of book now. He said, "Could we, do you think, loose this picture?" I said, "Lose it, you mean?" "They won't notice, they don't realise," he said, "this field would look better on your wall."

But the folder went back and the wheatfield with it. I forgot Ivan. I had to forget Ivan, for to remember Ivan meant remembering that room.

Now, I can remember the room for Bella moved down anyway, then Bella moved out.

The room is as it has been, as it always will be. I am sitting in the room now, but here the room is wider and has two doors. The couch is made up with its blue cover, under the slope of the roof. The floor isn't waxed because we can't get beeswax, but there is a feeling of a Dutch interior. There is a reflection in the surface of a polished table. It is the reflection of the rose-laurel branch in the jar, that Vincent painted.

It is not one of his important pictures. I don't know why I think of it now. But I remember it and an earlier upturned basket or pot of pansies.

Remembering Ivan, I remember the story. The story must have been there when I didn't go to your room. The story must have been part of my consciousness, though I didn't remember it. Vincent was locked up, in some place near Arles. He went on painting, half-crazy, when he got out. One of his later pictures was that very wheatfield (green-corn, he called it), showing the early green as the wind blew it. There are stiff sprays in the foreground. There is the distant roof of a farm-house like a ship on the waves. No, I am forcing this. I am trying to explain it. When I try to explain, I write the story. The story must write me, the story must create me. You are right about that great-mother, Elsa is like a wheatfield. But it's too complicated.

I can see it through your eyes, through Vincent's. You are driven by your genius. You will express love. Why does it drive you mad, that desire to create your mother?

He would get into the cypress tree, through his genius, through his daemon. Because of him alive in the cypress tree, alive in his mother, the cypress would be deified—not in the stylized classic manner, those very words repel me. It is worship, such as the Druids felt here with their sun-circle of stones. You talked of the dark-god, but there is nothing dark about it. I mean, there is nothing dark about Vincent's worship, though he was driven mad by it.

He might have stopped painting when he got out of the mad-house. But he couldn't do that. He went on with the green wheatfield and the last ripe wheatfield with the cypresses. Then he shot himself.

None of this was in my mind when I didn't come up to your room. But I would goad you on to writing, writing as Vincent painted.

I felt when I came here that the Phoenicians on the track from the mine to the sea, that you wrote me about, had left an imprint, not only the track past the Druid stones on the hill. The Druids left the same track or traces as Arthur did, Tintagel and his Druid round-table. The round-table or Arthur's Druid circle wasn't all warriors. There was Merlin. But I don't want to force parallels, comparisons. I have only just found out that you belong to that world. I have only just remembered.

I don't mean race-consciousness or reincarnation or anything like that. To try to explain it, spoils it, but I must try to explain. It was something that kept me from you.

I could not be your mother. Anyhow, I need a great-mother as much as you do.

The thing that kept me from you wasn't only your genius. I mean, it wasn't only your personal power and your way of writing. That bulky novel that you sent me had no doubt

the gold or the tin or whatever ore it was those Phoenicians
came to England to dredge out. I hadn't the strength nor
the equipment to dredge the ore out of the manuscript you
sent me. But I know it is there. It is in everything you write;
even if I don't agree with you or don't like what you're say-
ing. I know that the genius is there. I could only qualify or
differentiate you from the others, by saying you should write
as Vincent van Gogh painted.

There is a phrase sometimes or there was a sentence in
a letter that had that quality. And you see things as Vincent
saw them, that upturned pot or basket of pansies and those
old shoes.

He would draw that magnetism up out of the earth, he
did draw it. His wheat stalks are quivering with more than
the wind that bends them.

There is peace in the centre of the cyclone.

I don't really know if this man-is-man, woman-is-woman
means all that you think it does. I don't know that. I
couldn't have found it out, not then. I might find it out
later. But when it comes to loving a cypress or a peach-tree
as Vincent van Gogh loved them, one is going back, is going
forward. I mean, one is, as I said of myself with the candle
at my elbow, not yet born. Vincent is in the cypress, he is
in the blossoming fruit-tree, he is in the *gloire*.

Nature-worship doesn't express it, unless you see nature
as a Spirit. You said I was a living spirit, but I wasn't living
until you wrote to me, "We will go away together." We
have gone away together, I realise your genius, in this place.
I would like to serve your genius, not only because it is per-
sonally, your genius, but because it is part of this place.

I cannot see the future, but the war will be over sometime. I can think of London because of Ivan's room at the top of the house. I can think of the wide steps, the corridor and the wooden door opening on to the last narrow stair-case. I can think that you walked up those steps, that you slept there. I can remember breakfast the next morning. I can remember how you said to me, "You were singing in a dream. I woke and found my face wet with tears."